About the Author

Ben Lowe is a poet, novelist and environmentalist. He has had a few poems published. This is his first published novel.

He was inspired by the Club of Rome report in 1972 to become an environmentalist. This report was the first to show that the world's environment places limits on economic growth, and that we have to rethink how we live.

Ben is also a lawyer.

Ant Elope

Ben Lowe

Ant Elope

Olympia Publishers
London

www.olympiapublishers.com
OLYMPIA PAPERBACK EDITION

A CIP catalogue record for this title is
available from the British Library.

ISBN: 978-1-78830-818-2

This is a work of fiction.
Names, characters, places and incidents originate from the writer's
imagination. Any resemblance to actual persons, living or dead, is
purely coincidental.

First Published in 2021

Olympia Publishers
Tallis House
2 Tallis Street
London
EC4Y 0AB

Printed in Great Britain

Dedication

I wish to dedicate this novel to my sons, Max and Miki

Acknowledgements

I wish to express heartfelt thanks to a number of people who have made very helpful comments on my drafts, not least Pam Scobie, Lesley Glaister, Paul Redgrave, Nan Jackson, Andrea Findlay

Chapter 1
Bloody Owls

Hillsborough Stadium, Sheffield, UK

'Same old, same old.'

'Bloody Owls!'

'The so-called striker couldn't hit a barn door with a beachball.'

'Why do I pay good money every Saturday for this shit?'

'Awayawayaayawayaway...' the Kop crowd sings.

Then the song-chant: 'If you hate the fucking Blades fucking dance...'

This followed by an audible gasp, all round the South Stand, and the North Stand. Even the away end.

The Sheffield Wednesday Kop is empty.

Empty except for a few scarves and a few dozen programmes. And a walking stick — 8,000 people just gone — Disappeared.

The game stops. The players stand still. All 22. The referee the same. One or two players drop to their haunches and wipe away the odd tear with the back of the wrist.

There is an eerie uneasy silence. In this vast stadium, you can hear a pin drop.

'They've all gone for a slash out of boredom,' comes a cry from the South Stand.

'They heard Madonna was in the Park pub,' shouts another.

But for the rest, people are lost for words.

8,000 football fans gone in a flash.

Over the tannoy the club's announcer reports: 'In these highly exceptional circumstances, today's game has been abandoned. Please all leave now, but quietly, out of respect.'

The players and officials walk off the pitch, heads hung.

On their phones, fans leaving the stadium can see the TV footage being replayed. On the edge of the picture, there are fans one minute, and no fans the next minute. Unexplained, inexplicable.

The same pictures are coming from other stadia too: from St James' Park in Newcastle; from the Kop in Anfield, Liverpool, and the Etihad, Manchester, Stamford Bridge, Chelsea and Hawthorns, West Bromwich Albion.

Social media is abuzz with news of thousands disappearing from Las Ramblas in Barcelona, from a major festival in a central square in Perugia, Italy, from Red Square in Moscow, from the centre of Shanghai, from the Maracanã stadium in Rio, Brazil, from Boston, USA, and from a Hindi festival in Kolkata, India.

Mecca, Saudi Arabia

On the expansive square at the el Haj mosque in Mecca, Zara Mamood is cross:

'You have left out the humus, and the pitta bread. How can we have a picnic without the most basic ingredients?'

'I thought you had put them in already,' counters her husband Mahmud, defensively.

'Which is why they were on your list, I suppose. You will forget your head next, Mahmud.'

'I'm sorry. I didn't think.'

'What's new?'

'Here,' says a woman behind them, in full chador. 'We have some spare pitta bread,' and she hands them four pieces.

'No, we can't,' pleads Zara.

'Please, we are all sisters and brothers here.'

'Shokran, thanks,' says Mahmud.

A man drops his copy of the Koran as he passes. He kneels down and prays forgiveness for dropping the Holy Book. A man behind, his eyes looking up, falls over him. There are apologies all round.

Suddenly, the square is empty. Tens of thousands of people gone.

Just countless picnic tiffins and baskets, umpteen prayer mats, and numerous information leaflets flying in the gentle breeze.

As a large family enters the square, they stop and stare, dropping their bags. A square that should be full of tens of thousands of fellow Moslems, is completely bare, but for odd belongings that they have left behind.

. . .

The talk of aliens, spreads like wildfire.

Some begin talking of a strange sucking sound at the time of the disappearances. This goes viral on social media. The phenomenon of sucking becomes more and more exaggerated. On You Tube, the sucking theme gathers steam. Sucking sounds are reproduced in countless memes, accompanied by images of celebrities and well-known politicians disappearing.

There are no unusual sightings in the sky above the affected stadia, or Mecca or Shanghai, or in the sky anywhere.

Officially, the idea of aliens being behind the disappearances is dismissed as nonsense.

In each European country, the Prime Minister, President or Chancellor appears on television, but none offers an answer, and offers only a promise to stop at nothing to get the people back.

Some wonder if it is all an elaborate magic stunt; some say that they will simply all come back in a few hours, it is just a hoax; some talk of a time warp on a global scale.

The Spanish Government appoints a Disappearance Tsar, to analyse the disappearance in Barcelona and to report directly to the Prime Minister. Other countries follow suit, with specialists appointed.

In Washington, there is wide public discussion of the National Guard being despatched to various cities in readiness for further disappearances, but no action is taken.

On twitter, images slowed down to the slowest possible speed show, what appeared in the blur to be people going up. But even then, it is not at all clear where they go up to. The twitter-sphere is full of theories.

In a student common room in the Sussex University outside Brighton, different theories are proffered:

'Some magician's sleight of hand, I reckon.'

'No way. Not in so many places at once. Could be a trick of social media. Perhaps with a delay effect and inserting pictures from six in the morning, when all those places are empty.'

'Rubbish. People have been in the stadia and other places when it happened. They have seen it with their own eyes.'

'And look, there are images really slowed down which suggests people going up, but the image is quickly lost.'

'Well, there's no technology on Earth that can do that.'

'Unless it's a secret. Maybe NASA in the US, or the Russians, or the Chinese.'

'But the disappearing happens everywhere. Even in those countries.'

'That could be a cover, to make it look like it's not them.'

'Aliens is the best explanation.'

'But we know nothing about any aliens, so it explains nothing.'

'Could be a fifth-dimension phenomenon, a dimension of space.'

'Meaning what, clever dick?'

'Meaning that you and me are three dimensional. A drawing on a piece of paper is just two dimensions. If you add time, with its concepts of past, present and future, you have four dimensions. If you bring in space, with its infinite possibilities, you have the fifth dimension. Maybe those people have entered a fifth dimension, which is why we can't see them.'

'Too much information.'

'Can't get my head around people being there, and then not there. It's way outside my sense of reality.'

'Is it like *Sliding Doors*, that film with Gwyneth Paltrow?'

'Yea, that's all changing reality and stuff.'

'Well, that's not about the fifth dimension; it's about when fate is changed by nothing more than chance circumstances. You catch the train and these events happen;

you just miss the same train and this different chain of circumstances happen.'

'Maybe those poor disappeared guys missed the train.'

'Get real, Jeff, you're missing the point completely. This is not a film. It's deadly real.'

'Could be a spaceship collecting people for a planet where they need us to help.'

'Could be. Maybe they will take us as slaves, for some alien species.'

'Or maybe people have evolved on another planet to a higher level, but they need more people from here to do the basic jobs.'

'Likely story!'

'What do we know, really, all so weird.'

'Let's hope they don't all die.'

'My dad is one.'

'No! How come?'

'He was at Hillsborough, in the Kop, when all the Kop disappeared.'

'Have you heard anything?'

'I just got a text in the first half saying that Sheffield Wednesday were playing crap.'

'Has your mum heard anything?'

'They are not together. But his partner has heard nowt.'

'Must be hard for you.'

'Damned bloody hard not knowing. I'm as much in the dark as the rest of you.'

...

'Allah will know what to do', says one man, with high collar and tightly fitting suit.

He is drinking tea with a bunch of mates in an open-air cafe in Tehran, in the capital of Iran. They speak in Farsi.

'I think the CIA is behind it. It is always Amrika with its entrails everywhere in the world. They will have planned it all. Them or Mossad.'

'Mossad certainly, anything to sow discord amongst their enemies.'

'No, it will be the will of Allah. He will guide us when the time is right.'

'We have no idea where the people have gone to, whether they are alive or dead. It's so strange.'

'Reminds me of the days of the Shah. My grandparents say that thousands of people would just disappear, never to be seen again.'

'I don't think he's the culprit here, though. Unless his ghost has emerged from his grave.'

'We should think of the loved ones of those who have gone.'

'Allah may bring the lost ones back, just as he took them away. Maybe they are being punished for being infidels in all those infidel countries.'

'No, the CIA will be plotting it all. Everything will come out in time, just like when we invaded the US embassy in 1979. All the secrets and dirty tricks, and torture and murder, that we had imagined all proved to be true.'

'This is too strange, even for the CIA.'

'Let's see what the Ayatollah has to say.'

'Is he speaking?'

'Well, he never misses an opportunity.'

...

In a café garden in Santa Fe, New Mexico, USA, discussions
are lively.

'So spooky!'

'It's the maddest thing ever.'

'Must be the work of God.'

'God wouldn't do that.'

'The planet is too full, so he's taking people away.'

'Not God's way.'

'Alien abduction, I say. What else can it be?'

'You see too many bad B movies, Tork.'

'Don't you guys feel sorry for these people? They might
all be dead.'

'Aw, we can't worry about what we don't know.'

'My techie brother has sent me this link. I'm forwarding
it to you. Shows they defo went up.'

'God's work, I tell you.'

'No way, alien abduction.'

'It'll be a parallel universe. There is our universe, and this
other one alongside. People can shift from one to the other.'

'No way!'

'I reckon that is where these people are, living in a
different universe. One day they may come back.'

'It's like *Being John Malkovich*.'

'What, you mean when they go inside his head, and
there's a different world there? Cool. I liked that.'

'The guy who wrote that has this funny story; he was out
jogging, and going down this hill, and he passes a much older

jogger, huffing and puffing up the hill, and the older jogger turns and says to him: "it's all downhill that way".'

'I like that, funny.'

'It's a nice joke, and a good film, but nothing to do with a parallel universe.'

'I don't know about other universes. I reckon it's those guys in Los Alamos down the road who are up to something. They hid those aliens back in the 1950s. They know everything about aliens, but it's all top secret. There is even film of the aliens.'

'Do you know where they went?'

'No, they were disappeared very quickly. But it's the same with the Mecca people, and the Rio people. They were there one minute, gone the next.'

'I think I'll just have some magic mushrooms. It's better to hallucinate than face reality.'

'Maybe God's been eating magic mushrooms.'

'That's sacrilegious! You can't say that.'

'I can say what I like. I think I'll have a hash cake too. Good idea.'

'Maybe all the disappeared will be eating hash cake with the aliens.'

'Don't make fun of it, Zeke, these people might all be dead, the poor fuckers.'

...

In Cape Town, South Africa, a bunch of friends on the waterfront are relaxing over a drink. Their conversation shifts from Zulu to English and back.

'This is like the apartheid era, guys, people disappearing left, right and centre.'

'I reckon it's BOSS just like then, trying to frighten everyone so they can get power for the whities again.'

'They would stop at nothing. But would they do things in all those other countries? How would they?'

'They and Mossad would work together, just like in those ugly kill-all-the-blacks times.'

'I think it's too much even for them. Shanghai, Boston, Rio.'

'It will be God's will. It will part of his plan.'

'But there is nothing in the Bible about abducting people in huge numbers.'

'God does not only follow the Good Book.'

'Must be aliens. What else can it be?'

'Rubbish. Aliens are just science fiction.'

'Our ancestors will be spooked about all the wrongs in the world. Maybe our ancestors are taking people to the underworld.'

'Yea, why not? Our ancestors have been quiet for a long time.'

'Our ancestors would curse all the people doing this.'

'Maybe that's it then, a curse. Our ancestors telling us the evil of our ways.'

'Forget that mumbo jumbo. God's will is behind this.'

'You're all talking out of your backsides, guys. I'm leaving.'

Chapter 2
The Spaceship, Part 1

For the disappeared, there is a strange new world to experience.

They land on a wide metal grill in a cavernous hall, bounded by metal walls, landing with a multiple thud, a clatter, in a large pile. Those atop try to climb down, some leap. There is universal chaos.

They shout scream bellow swear.

My glasses, where are my glasses? Where the fuck are we? Where's Charlie? Charlie, shout to me if you can hear me. Irene, where are you? Giuseppe, hold my hand, get the fuck off my arm; ouch, my leg.

Over and over.

Expletives in every dialect, every language, every shade of blue.

Panic as people look and shout for loved ones.

Then an overwhelming sense of anguish, confusion, as more and more realise that the metallic grill they have landed on is covered in a sticky substance, like a fly trap.

They squirm, and wriggle and struggle and vainly tear at the substance.

The more that they battle to free themselves, the more they become stuck to the icky sticky material that covers the grill.

One shouts: 'Make a bridge, all of you, I am still free, I will climb over you.'

And, as a few dozen lie flat he steps gingerly on to their bodies.

'Oy, watch my boobies,' shouts one.

'Ouch, my balls,' screams another.

'Fuck, that hurt!' says a third.

But the would-be runaway soon runs out of bodies, accidentally steps on the grill, and becomes ensnared himself.

Across from this group, which is mainly British, another large number of bodies tumble down on to another part of the grate.

Now more screams, shouts, expletives, this time mainly in German:

'Verdammt noch mal; Arschloch.'

'Was ist denn das, um Gottes Willen!?'

And then another clatter of thousands of bodies, with a continuous sound of Arabic screams and wails.

A shadow falls across the huddled, muddled, befuddled mass. An ant-shaped elongated shadow.

An enormous robotic ant stands on its back two legs and casts its eyes over the multitude.

'I am Reson,' it booms. 'You will lie still. To struggle is pointless.'

And the same repeated in German, Spanish, Arabic, Italian, French, Punjabi.

'What about my kids? I need to collect my kids,' shouts one.

'My dad's dying, I must get there,' screams another.

'Me too,' shouts a middle-aged woman, 'my mum's dying. Please please let me go.'

'I've just broken my arm falling in here!'

'I've done my leg in!'

'I've got a job interview tomorrow. My life depends on it.'

'Fat chance,' shouts another.

'You will live about three or four days in your human time dimension,' says Reson, flatly, in each of the languages.

'Three or four fucking days?!' exclaim a hundred or more, almost in unison, and this is repeated by each language group, almost like a round, as they hear the robot.

'It's inhuman!' bellows one.

'It's very human, if you reflect for a moment. Humans kill each other all the time. And kill creatures. The difference with your killing of creatures is that when you kill ants or other creatures you don't wait at all. You just kill,' replies Reson in a booming voice.

'Who gives a monkey's toss about ants?!' screams one.

'What have we done to deserve this?' shouts a Geordie.

'What do you think?!' screams back a diminutive young woman, her spiky hair streaked yellow and black, ring in nose, skin between cinnamon and light chestnut.

'You mean because we have treated ants badly?' asks the Geordie.

'Yeah, what's so bad about killing ants?' says another.

'It isn't just ants,' retorts the spiky-haired woman, 'it's all animals, from the dodo, to the black rhino, the African elephant, the blue whale, and so many other creatures either extinct or near extinction.'

'Who the fuck are you?', asks an irate Sheffielder.

'Olga,' says the spiky-haired woman.

'It is your planet,' comes the powerful voice of Reson. 'You have put your planet in jeopardy, you have been foolhardy, reckless.

'Several of our species are at risk because of the damage you have done. The survival of the planet as a home for our cousins is at risk. Because of your species. You don't deserve to live as a species.'

'How many of us are here?' asks a concerned voice.

'Humans count things, ants worry little about numbers,' says Reson, 'but we robots are programmed to understand your numbers.'

'It must be thousands,' says one, craning her neck all around.

'There are seven more decks like this on the craft,' says Reson.

'You are raving bonkers,' says the Geordie.

'Where do we all come from?' asks a Sheffielder in blue and white.

'Fucking Newcastle!' shouts another Geordie.

'De Barcelona!' shouts a football fan with a Barcelona FC shirt.

'Mecca!' screams an Arab woman.

'We have taken from football stadia,' says the ant robot, 'and from festivals, public prayers in some countries, and also city centres, where large numbers gather. When humans crowd, we can take big numbers very easily.'

'More likely tens of thousands,' shouts a German, from across the way.

'Where are we?' asks a Scot.

'You are in a spaceship,' bellows Reson. 'When it is full, we shall leave.'

'Leave to where?' asks the Sheffielder.

'Don't worry,' says Reson, 'you'll all be long dead by the time we get there. It's in another galaxy.'

'Fuck me sideways!' exclaims the Scot.

'When you said we don't to deserve to survive, what did you mean?' asks a Frenchman.

'He said we don't deserve it as a species,' says the German.

'You have caused such terrible damage to the planet you inhabit. says Reson. We will see to it that humans cease to damage the planet, and then other species, not least ants, will take over the planet, and help it to heal.'

'But that's terrible,' shouts a red-haired woman.

'We must warn people,' says a spiky-haired young man, reaching for his mobile.

'No phones or human computers will work in here,' says Reson.

'Oh my God, I will go cold turkey without my ipad.'

'Join the real world,' shouts the Sheffielder.

'How will we eat?' asks an elderly man.

'And how will we shit?' asks the woman next to him.

'You will shit where you are. You will survive with what is in your stomachs for a time,' says Reson, 'after that you will slowly die.'

'You can't just let us all die like that!' screams a silver-haired, well-coiffured man, 'I've got a bank to run. Huge numbers of people rely on me.'

'I'm getting out of here,' says a woman in her wheelchair, but she is no better able to move than anyone else.

'We need a plan,' shouts a Geordie.

'We can't all lie here and die like animals,' shouts a Brummie woman.

A hum starts up, grows louder, becomes more a whoop, then a howl, and fills the whole cavernous space, reverberating round the walls.

'Stop! Now!' Reson booms out. The powerful sound slowly subsides.

'We can kill you all, and we will. Welcome to the world of insects and animals. But I can assure that some of you won't be left to die,' says Reson.

'What will happen to them?' asks the Brummie.

'They will be killed quickly,' said Reson, 'we need energy for the spaceship, and for me and my colleagues.'

'What the fuck!' shouts the Scot, 'are we just fuel for bloody ants?'

'You never thought about our species when you trod on one of our carefully built homes, with half a million ants inside, or when you sprayed us with poison,' shouts Reson, showing no emotion.

'Is this payback time?' asks the German.

'You misunderstand,' booms Reson, 'we are a far more advanced species than you. We have travelled many light years, using robots like me.'

'Light years. Never!'

'This is far beyond what your species can do. The use of your species as fuel is on the one hand an efficient use of resources, on the other a way of starting to cleanse your planet of a highly toxic and dangerous species.'

'You are having me on,' says the Sheffielder. 'You are telling me that ants built this spaceship? Jesus, man, pull the other one.'

'Ants have been a superior species since long before your species started on the Blue Planet, since the time you were just monkeys,' counters Reson. 'We have seen your species from its early days, and in these early years it was a kindly species, living in harmony with other species.'

'"Blue Planet", where is that?' asks Olga.

'That's our planet, I reckon,' opines the Scot, 'it looks blue when filmed from space.'

A German wriggles out of his overcoat, pulls his legs out of his trousers, and jumps up. '*Ik bin frei!*' he exclaims, in a Berlin accent.

A woman struggles out of her dress and jumps up also, and a boy who has left his coat and jeans behind, each piece of clothing stuck to the grate like the clothes of the others.

They move towards each other, as they seek to cross the grate and meet each other, but one by one their feet become stuck on the grate when they slip off the side of bodies. The boy lies down and cries, and a woman consoles him.

Reson is not impressed: 'Let all of you be warned. There is no escape from this craft.'

And is if to re-emphasise the point, another large number of bodies arrives in the chamber, on the other side of the Germans. As with the earlier arrivals, the newcomers scrabble to get down from the pile, and express anguish, anger and confusion in equal measure.

Oleg and Reson

'I can help you,' says Olga, looking up at the giant robot.

'I don't think so,' says Reson.

'I can be your ambassador to the humans.'

'No thanks,' replies Reson.

'Why are you called Reson?' asks Olga.

'Reson Ant. Just like Eleg Ant, Blat Ant, and so on. It makes it easier for the humans, we think.'

'Well, I could help with your programming. Bring it more up to date.'

'More up to date?' asks Reson.

'Yes,' says Olga. 'English is always evolving. More American words, more tech words, more slang words, phrases from social media and so on. It could help you to have up-to-date English.'

'Maybe,' says Reson.

'Maybe what?' asks Olga.

'Maybe you could help, but there is a catch.'

'OK. What is the catch?' asks Olga, now very curious.

'We do take a few helpers, but they may have to mate.'

'Mate? Do you mean fuck each other?'

'I mean have babies, which involves mating.'

'And if I say no?' asks Olga.

'Then you may have a more onerous task.'

'And if I do it, can I choose who I mate with?' asks Olga.

'We are in control here,' says Reson, coldly.

'OK, I get it. What happens to the children?' asks Olga.

'They are mostly used for our fuel,' says Reson, but some are kept on for the same purpose many years on, for further breeding.'

'Pretty grotesque,' says Olga.

'But you may be excused from this,' says Reson.

'Do I escape from this sticky grate?' asks Olga.

'If we choose you,' says Reson.

'I volunteer,' says the Geordie.

'And me,' says the man next to him, also with a Geordie accent.

'And me,' comes a chorus of men and women all around.

Reson turns around and walks away.

'Fuck off the lot of you,' shouts Olga to all around her who could hear.

'I will mate with you,' says a tall Sheffielder, with a wink.

'I'm not that desperate,' chuckles Olga, looking him up and down.

There is a chorus of 'if you hate the fucking ants clap your hands' from a large group of blue and white clad Sheffielders, a number of whom have hands free to clap with; and before long most of those in blue and white are joining in, all of them football supporters.

The chant is taken up by an even larger group of Geordies in black and white, also football fans. It becomes quite deafening. Then dies away almost as soon as it started.

Reson returns to Olga a little later. It sprays from one finger around her body and lifts her up with the other upper robotic hand. She looks at Reson half cautiously, but half triumphantly, feeling that she has been chosen.

Reson strides to the edge of the chamber and places Olga in a small box. This has very little light but has a few holes, which allow in some of the artificial light from the chamber.

In the box is some raw cabbage and carrots. Olga first puts her nose close to these and smells each cautiously, and then starts to chew on a carrot, deeply relieved to have something.

The air is clammy in the box, but she can breathe.

Suddenly, another robot ant lifts the box's lid and peers in.

'I am told you are going to help programme us?' the ant says.

'Yes, I think so,' replies Olga, 'but what is your name?'

'For you I am Eleg,' says the robot.

From the vantage point she has Olga cannot not tell whether 'Eleg Ant' is appropriate or not. This ant seems much like Reson.

'Give me some phrases,' says Eleg. 'I can store them and feed them into our programme. We need new phrases, and new words, so that we can communicate with your strange species.'

'I don't know off hand,' replies Olga, a little caught by surprise at how quickly her idea has been taken up, 'but try this for starters. A silly short poem by Spike Milligan to start us off. It goes:

There are holes in the sky
where the rain gets in
but they're ever so small
that's why the rain is so thin.'

'But this is not true,' replies Eleg.

'It is a nonsense poem, a bit of humour,' says Olga, 'I can help you with humour for starters.'

'Can you give me something more for everyday use?' asks Eleg.

'What about the phrase "come out" to start with? This can mean simply, leave the house with you; or it can mean to declare oneself publicly in support of a cause or an idea; and it can now very commonly mean declaring oneself publicly to be a homosexual.'

'Homosexual we know, and we have other words: gay, faggot, poofter,' says Eleg.

'I suggest you delete poofter from your programme, and also faggot, which is not often used now,' says Olga.

'What else?' asks Eleg.

'We say "in the closet" for a gay person who has not come out,' says Olga, warming to her theme.

'Why would a human not want to say he was gay? Our species do not have such distinctions. This is all new to me,' asks Eleg.

'Too complicated,' says Olga, trying to move away from a tricky subject. 'How about "skitch", which describes hanging on to a car or truck while riding on a skateboard.'

'Stop', says Eleg, 'there is too much in that for me. I will need to understand what is happening. Car… skateboard… riding…'

The noise outside the box suddenly erupts again, with a growing crescendo from several groups of football supporters singing, 'we are the champions, we are the champions.'

The Germans join in too, and then also the French, so that the sound fills the whole cavernous area.

Reson's voice booms out: 'Quiet now. The craft is departing. You need to be still, otherwise the force could break your necks, which you may find uncomfortable. Very uncomfortable.'

There is a hushed silence. Nobody finds it at all funny.

'We are human till we die… we are human till we die,' starts a new chant, amongst the black and white shirted supporters, based on a football chant. 'Oh humans, we are human till we die…' and the chant spreads across to all the different groups, with the Germans and French and some Italians also joining in, in their own languages.

The Arabs are mainly in prayer, but cannot adopt their usual posture, and remain lying down, like most of the people in the craft.

The sound from the repeated chant of 'we are human till we die' becomes almost overpowering, as thousands join in, but in time the volume drops until it eventually dies away.

The lighting in the craft is reduced. There is just the minutest glimmer coming through from the stars through tiny portholes.

The craft's movement is so silent that nobody noticed it has started its flight.

'How fast will the craft fly?' asks Olga.

'We fly quite fast until we go round your planet's moon, then we flip round this to double our speed, which will then be around half the speed of light...'

'What, flip around? How does that work?'

'We use the gravitational pull of the moon, so that we can travel round in its orbit, and we can obtain a whip-like effect as we emerge on the other side and break out of its orbit.'

'Knock me sideways!' exclaims Olga.

'And then we flip round the little planet you call Mars and through that we reach the speed of light. That is our maximum speed. For the time being.'

'Have we left yet?' asks a Geordie.

'Fucked if I know,' responds his next-door neighbour.

'Must have, though, I guess,' says the first.

Olga turns to Eleg: 'I will tell you a bit about the word "skitch" if you want, and skateboards.'

Eleg looks at Olga: 'Can we look at words that may be more useful to us robots when talking to your strange species in the English language?'

'OK, how about "Yolo", which may be apt here.'

'What is "Yolo"?'

'It means "You only live once". You take the first letter of each word. We call this technique an acronym.'

'"Yolo". Very good. I can say this to the humans who try to play daft with me.'

'Play silly buggers,' Olga suggested.

'OK, slay billy puggers.'

'Not quite,' said Olga, 'but it sounds just as good. How tall are you? You are like a giraffe, nearly as big as a giraffe.'

Eleg says, 'Tall enough, we don't have measurements like you.'

'You're like a crane.'

'A bird?' asks Eleg.

'No, a mechanical crane for making buildings.'

'OK. I prefer a bird comparison.'

Chapter 3
The Spaceship, Part 2

'Chocolate. He's got chocolate!' shouts Ray. 'Hey you. Share it out. We're all starving here!'

'It's my chocolate, and I'll eat it,' says the Sheffielder.

'And that woman's got crisps!' shouts another.

'We should all live together and die together,' insists Ray, 'everyone with food should share it out.'

One woman struggles out of her dress and leaps toward the chocolate eater, grabbing it from him, breaking a piece and passing the rest on to a neighbour, who does the same.

Now a number of women rip off dresses to escape the grill, and clamber around searching for food.

Spotting this, a number of men and boys try to struggle out of coats and trousers to break free.

Soon, a few dozen men, and two boys, are crawling over the bodies, searching in pockets.

'I've found water,' says a Geordie, 'here, you have some,' and he passes it on.

'I've found two half-eaten bags of peanuts, and a Twix,' crows a woman, with beaming smile.

'Heh, they are mine!' screams a girl, crying.

Hands grab for them. The woman passes them on, ignoring the girl's tears.

A few of the freed crawlers try to get right across the mass of bodies, for no reason other than to have a moment of relative freedom.

But soon a shadow looms over them.

Reson booms out: 'Nobody gets free here. And there is nowhere to go. Go back immediately!'

Some reluctantly turn back and retrace their steps — or their handprints in most cases. But a few stand their ground.

One boy suddenly slides across a few bodies on a plastic jacket. 'Watch me skitch,' he says.

Reson strides across, reaches out, and picks up the boy. 'What's your name?'

'Alf,' says the lad.

'Is this a skitch?' asks Reson.

'Not really, I was just improvising,' says Alf, shocked that the robot knows about skitching.

'Well, this is me improvising,' and Reson throws Alf past several bodies, until he lands clumsily.

'Fucking hell,' says the woman he lands on.

'Not my fucking fault,' moans Alf, rubbing his bruises. And his pride.

Reson then raises a leg and fires a white substance at the remaining would-be rebels. It lands on its targets immediately and their faces are covered with a gooey substance. They collapse, their bodies now rigid, unable to move even a muscle.

'Those who do not obey will be paralysed immediately,' says Reson.

'We are humans, we are humans, we are humans till we die,' rises the chant again.

And again, the chant spreads through the vast chamber, taken up by many of the different nationalities, in several languages. It resonates around.

Reson turns around and walks back to where it has previously stood. Its back is turned briefly.

Now a few Arabs come forward, climbing over people who have been paralysed by the sticky substance.

There has been no noise for a while from the thousands of Arabs. They all seemed to be praying.

Gradually, more and more women are taking off their outer garments, almost all chadors, and more and more men are doffing djellaba or tunics or overshirts.

They lay the outer garments as though they are creating a large carpet and now, having morphed into an active coordinated mass in white undergarments, they start moving in the direction of the robot Reson.

Others start to assist. The doffed garments that are no longer needed and which are not stuck down are passed over heads to the front, so that those attempting some kind of escape could keep on moving forward.

The throng repeats over and over '*Allah o Akbar*'.

Again, and again, Reson raises a leg and sprays those coming nearer to it. But the numbers seem to confuse Reson. The robot is not quite prepared for such a large rebellion. It begins to retreat a little, still spraying.

A large group of Germans, who soon realise what is happening, see that the Arabs need to pass over them to continue onwards, and most lay flat. A few, who find this to be possible, take off shirts and trousers, or skirts or dresses, and join the Arabs.

So a large group of Arabs, plus a few Germans, proceed in an impressive glacier-like mass towards Reson, who stands tall and calls out in Arabic:

'You will stop there! Now!' The Arabs remain silent but continue. Those at the front are now almost upon Reson.

Reson raises a finger and shoots his sticky liquid at all the Arabs at the front of the huge group approaching. Their faces freeze, their limbs become powerless.

'Stop now, or you will all be paralysed!' shouts Reson, who now puts one upper leg to its shoulder and presses a blue button.

The Arabs behind ignore Reson and move closer, until Reson fires the sticky liquid at the next row. In this way, Arabs are being placed in some kind of frozen state by the hundred, but those behind them are still able to move forward, scrambling over or around those paralysed.

Suddenly, they are at Reson's legs, and Reson fires as much liquid as it can at those all around. As Reson starts to topple, Eleg comes forward and sprays liquid over the numerous Arabs closest to Reson.

There is now chaos as Reson falls prone to the floor, and dozens of Arabs collapse all round, affected by the robot spray, paralysed and powerless.

Eleg keeps spraying the Arabs behind, whose first inclination is to continue forward, only to find that the sheer number of Arabs who are now paralysed in random body positions makes it impossible for them to advance from any direction.

Slowly most of the remaining unparalysed Arabs retreat to the area they had come from, gathering up what outer garments that they can on their way.

The Germans, who had already retreated, start to cheer the Arabs. Brits re-start the chant of 'we are humans till we die', while also applauding, and this spreads around the cavernous space.

Eleg now lifts Reson across to the sliding door area where Eleg first came in. There, handholds are available, and Reson is able to stand up again.

Reson and Eleg stand and face the dishevelled bodies in front of them

'All of you go back now, or you will die in seconds!' Reson booms.

This time, almost all the remaining rebelling humans retreat, except for those paralysed or who have again become stuck on the grill. Just a handful stand their ground, but Reson fires the sticky substance at their faces, so they will be unable to breathe. Now there are no more willing to face instant paralysis, and the retreat continues.

Reson moves across to the box where Olga is. She is still a bit bewildered about what has just happened.

Reson speaks first:

'We are going to move things forward a bit now, after the episode that has taken place. You will need a companion soon, and I will attend to this. The people on this level have no right to live until their bodies cease to function. We will use our faster method.'

'What is the faster method?' asks Olga.

'You will see,' says Reson. 'Our friends in the insect world have a role to play. But first I will bring a companion to you.'

Reson moves across to where there is a large number of Swedes, who are mainly wearing yellow and blue football-related outfits. Reson stretches out two long upper legs, and lifts up a squirming, moaning young man, dark hair, stubble moustache, beard, and brings him over to the box, where he is slowly lowered down next to Olga. He is a little smaller than Olga, and plumper.

He looks a little perplexed.

'I'm Olga,' she says. 'Do you speak English?'

'I'm Christer, and I can speak some English. Yes,' he says. 'Do you speak German?'

'I do,' she replies. 'But let's stick to English, otherwise I could get in a right tangle.'

'What do you make of this craft?' asks Christer. 'I sense they've got us hook, line and splinter.'

'Sinker,' Olga corrects. 'Hook, line and sinker. But I agree. I just want to go with the flow and see what happens.'

'Do you have a sense as to why the two of us have been separated out?' asks Christer.

'I have been asked to help them update their speech software, and maybe they'll ask the same of you, for their Swedish or possibly their German,' says Olga.

'That's no big deal,' says Christer. 'But it doesn't sound a big enough justification for these robots and their masters to travel such great distances. They must be from a very long way away in the galaxy.'

'Well, you guess right,' she says. 'They told me their planet is many light years away from Planet Earth. But there's a catch.'

'OK, what's the catch?'

'I think you are my mating companion,' quips Olga. 'And you get vegetables as a special bonus.' And she hands him a carrot, which he takes gratefully.

'Hopefully we can take some time to get to know each other,' says Christer. 'Or do they want us to fuck like rabbits, and do so without delay?'

'Who knows?' replies Olga. 'But let's chat for a bit, either way. This place is about as sexy as a morgue. Don't you find this all a bit spooky?'

'Spooky?'

'Weird, strange. The ant robots, the spaceship.'

'I guess,' he says. 'You don't think there are television cameras somewhere? Some kind of off the wall TV reality show? I mean it's not likely, but I find the idea of the ant robots running a spaceship a bit much.'

'It's real, right enough,' replies Olga. 'They are cleaning up planet Earth and taking away loads of humans as punishment for all the damage we have done to the earth.'

'I don't like the idea of taking so many people,' says Christer. 'I vote Green in Sweden. I limit the plastic I use and drive a car only rarely. All this is a bit extreme....'

'What's that noise?' asks Olga, abruptly.

'You're right,' answers Christer, 'it's a kind of nibbling. A lot of nibbling. Bizarre!'

Then the screams start. Just a few at first. Then thousands are shrieking and shouting.

The sound is bloodcurdling, so high a register that it could burst an eardrum.

Olga curls up on the floor and blocks her ears with hands and knees, so excruciating is the noise. Christer stands there with glazed eyes. Uncomprehending.

'Get the damned things off my face,' shouts one person.

'Yuk, they've got inside my pants!'

'Get out, you bastards, get out!'

'Aaargh, they're in my hair!'

'Whatever I do, I can't get them off me, they're chewing my neck now.'

'Bloody Arabs, they brought this on us.'

'Well, we supported them.'

'Fucking evil things, there are millions of them!'

'Aaaagghh. I can't get them off my eyes.'

The screams grow in volume and intensity.

There is general pandemonium and blind panic.

Most are unable to free themselves from the grill they are adhered to, but a few try to undress, a bit like the Arabs. In vain. The insects are inside their underclothes too.

Arms flail, feet kick out, trying to deal with the invasion, but it is a losing battle.

It remains a deafening, piercing, ear-splitting sound that fills the whole space.

As the worst of the screaming starts to subside, Olga gets up and calls to Reson to come over.

'What is happening?' she asks.

'We have introduced our friends the cockroaches to these people,' replies Reson. 'This breed is particularly fond of human flesh.'

'And you are killing everybody this way?' asks Christer.

'Most will die this way. Not you or the others in boxes. Some may die naturally, of heart attacks and so on. Normally, the cockroaches are introduced when the people are all dead, as they turn the bodies into excellent fuel. But on this occasion, the people have been so disobedient that we brought our friends in earlier. The bodies will still become fuel, of course.'

'It is a spectacle, and a sound, that will live with me forever, for the wrong reasons.'

'Indeed! The sound especially, the screams coming from deep within, like a strangled cat, they are frightening, almost blood-curdling,' says Olga, lowering her eyes.

'Well, I suppose you will say they brought it upon themselves,' surmises Christer.

'They chose an early death,' says Reson. 'So yes. They disobeyed, so they brought forward their deaths.' It walks off.

A subdued moaning and screaming goes on almost interminably, it seems, but gradually it subsides.

Christer goes to a corner of the box and sits with arms hugging his knees and his forehead resting on his arms. He shuts his eyes. Olga is aware of sobs emerging from his direction.

Sometime later, Christer emerges from deep contemplation. He wipes away the odd tear.

Olga is deep in thought, but not visibly upset. She wonders whether she should have strong feelings about what she has seen, or whether it is OK to feel nothing, as she does now.

Christer looks up at her.

'Does none of this affect you?' he asks her.

'I had a strange upbringing in Kerala, India, with a Danish-German father and Buddhist mother. We were ostracised. At school, I was isolated, with no friends except a mangy dog. At some point, I learnt to block all emotions out. This stayed with me when I later moved to Europe with my father.'

'Can you not even feel for someone in a relationship?'

'No. No feeling. I have never had therapy, so I don't know why. I have come to accept it.'

Christer casts his eyes around outside the box, horror-struck.

Most humans outside their box lie in contorted positions, apparently lifeless; many limbs have been severed.

Smaller metre-high ant robots, each with a huge metal sweep, begin to brush up the mass of human remains. It is a long process, with so many bodies.

'Messy business. It's a bastard to witness,' replies Olga.

'I feel sick,' replies Christer. 'I'm going to try to sleep. It's too hard to talk to you after this.'

As he wakes, a few hours later, Olga is standing next to him.

'It's all rather sudden and direct, I grant you, all this killing, but the Buddhist in me tells me we have to think about how we act as a species.'

And as she is speaking, she notices in the corner of her eye another man in a box, on the far side, black and striking, and deep in conversation with Eleg.

'Fuck off, Olga. You are brutal, do you know that? At least let me wake first.'

'Sorry.'

Christer sits and ponders a while, then looks up:

'I think it's over the top to talk of human behaviour, given what's just happened,' says Christer. 'We are trying to go greener where I live, cut down the growth of greenhouse gases, move towards renewable energy...'

'But it's too little too late,' retorts Olga, starting get into her stride. 'The earth is in a tailspin. The rate of damage is increasing too rapidly.'

'In what way?'

'Look at the Antarctic, the rate of decline in the ice is exponential. This is changing the global climate, raising sea levels, all with catastrophic knock-on events.'

'We don't know that. The earth's temperature has changed over time, when you look back millions of years. It is possible that Earth will adapt to these current rises in temperature. Besides that, you are such a cold fish, Olga. All those people die in front of you and you want to talk about saving the planet.'

'It's horrible, gross, and very hard to witness. But I have some weird condition. I don't have emotions like others.'

'OK.'

'The question is: why is all this happening on Earth? You talk of natural rises in the earth's temperature. There has not been a rise like this while there has been a large human population, and we know now from numerous scientific reports that humans have caused the current rise that is causing such insurmountable problems. Humans have put the planet in this position, and we have put many species at risk in the process.'

'That is too sweeping a conclusion. There are many organisations protecting species. And many creatures whose population has shrunk to a few dozen individuals are being kept alive and being helped to breed. You dismount all this good work.'

'Do you mean discount?'

'Yes. Discount.'

'It is chicken feed. Trillions of insects have died in recent years. Bees, which do so much to pollinate our crops, are at risk; many insect species have been wiped out, as have many animal species.'

'Well, I think you are mixing up climate change and the risk posed to other species. They are not necessarily linked. And, when it comes to climate change, countries like Sweden and Norway are doing a lot to reduce emissions and change how we live. It is major economies, not least the USA and China, that are causing most of the damage, and what can we do about them?'

'Well, you know. I think it is all linked. It all seems to have started after a creature appeared on earth, through evolution. When that creature, homo sapiens, eventually learnt to harness the energy from carbon resources found underground, oil, gas and coal, this creature began the process of destroying the environment of the planet it inhabited.'

'Isn't that rather over the top?'

'I don't think so. We are the first species to destroy the environment we need to live in. We are a creature with a powerful brain, but we are brainless, because we undermine our potential for survival by our own stupid actions. We are the brainless brainies, the Braibies.'

'I think that is a logical phrase, which I will log,' says Eleg, leaning down, having just returned to this side of the ship.

'Who said you could listen in?' asks Olga.

'I do sometimes as I need to know what is happening so better to control this ship.'

'I am happy for you to listen,' says Christer, 'I hope you agree, Eleg, that humans are not so bad. That we have contributed a lot to the planet we inhabit.'

'You are in a house,' says Eleg, 'a good house that has been standing proud for centuries. In the past years — I think

60 of your years — you have made the roof rotten and the roof now leaks.'

'You mean the ozone layer, the rise in carbon emissions?' asks Christer.

'The rise in carbon emissions, yes. You have also made the walls of the house porous, killed many of the insects in the house, and undermined the structure so that it is crumbling apart. If you are not stopped, you will also weaken the floors so that you fall through.'

'Clever metaphor, and I agree that much bad has happened,' says Christer, 'but the eco-warriors would have us give up cars, planes, oil, plastic — the world as we know it. We can't do that.'

'It is more serious than that,' says Eleg. 'Humans are currently committing collective suicide in the way you are managing the Blue Planet. You do have the right to do this, but you do not have the right to take other creatures with you, and we will not allow that. We will protect all those that need protecting. Ants on your planet tell us that their habitat is more under threat now than ever before, in all the 130 million years they have been on Earth.'

'I had no idea,' says Christer, 'but you don't see ant numbers declining. There are still ants in the places you expect to see ants.'

'There are many ants. There are more than a million ants for every human being, for every Brainless Brainy, or Braiby, as Olga calls you. 'But a trillion have died in recent times. If ants keep declining at the rate they have been declining in recent times, our position on Earth will become perilous. This is the same position with many of our relatives, such as bees and wasps.'

'Bees and wasps? Your relatives!?' exclaims Christer.

'You know little, like most Braibies. Ants started when some bees lost their wings. Many ants still have wings when we are young. but we have changed in character in all this time, so don't look the same as bees.'

'And don't sting as much,' adds Olga.

'Most ants have a sting, but not as toxic as the bee sting. I will introduce you to the bees on board later in the trip; they give us food for you and wax we need and other things.'

'What do you say, Christer, can you now see how even a highly numerous species like ants is being threatened by what humans are doing to the planet?'

'I can see there is damage, but I am not convinced how much it is down to human action. But I'm ducking out of this conversation now. My brain hurts.'

....

Chimananda and Souad

There are two women in another box across the cavernous space from Olga and Christer. One, Souad, has a fresh open face, with facial hair above her top lip and next to her ears (a man's sideburn area); she is medium height for a woman, and has a lively personality and a ready smile. She is a Christian Arab from Baghdad; Chimananda is tall and slender, with skin more purple-black than ebony. She has a mass of tightly curled hair, which encircles her face very strikingly. She has a ready smile. She is from Lagos, Nigeria.

'I find all this a bit overpowering. I don't know about you,' says Souad.

'For me, it reminds me of being crowded into a stinky, sweaty, dirty pen by Nigerian military.'

'Sounds heavy.'

'It's difficult being eco in Nigeria. All the oil revenue has gone to the "fuck you we'll take what we want" multinational oil companies, or the corrupt "keep quiet or I'll have your fucking tongue for breakfast" Nigerian elite, mostly military top brass. The mass of the people, get next to nothing.

'Lots of us want to harness the power of the sun in Nigeria, the offshore wind off the coast, and tidal energy, so that all the people can benefit, but we get stamped on like flies.'

'It's even worse in Iraq. The eco movement can't even get past first base. There were the years of post-Saddam war, and then the years of fanatical ISIS controlling huge chunks of the country, and having an eco blind-spot, then the years of incompetent political leaders from one religious persuasion or another, again with an eco blind-spot.'

'I can't believe you lived through all that.'

'You try to get up, go to school, learn, come home for tea, but the next you know half the roof is blown off your school, and you are relocated to a half-bombed hotel that has been vacated. The teachers improvise, do their best, but many of their teaching materials go up in smoke, and we just have to get by best we can.'

'Sounds crazy.'

'The best thing was having dance lessons in the hotel ballroom, space to twirl and jiggle in and with big mirrors to see how ugly you are. The mirrors were all cracked, but it was still a bit special.'

'You are not ugly.'

'I'm hairy where a woman shouldn't be, have no waist, have thick calves. No man has ever looked at me.'

'You are gorgeous. You have a smile that could light up a room. You have a delightful personality.'

'Thanks, but I know the truth of it. After school, I tried to get out of Iraq, and applied for a university place near Beirut, Lebanon.'

'Another war-torn country?'

'It was paradise compared to Iraq, by then. The worst of the civil war was over, and there was a sort of uneasy peace. I got into Jounieh's Holy Spirit University, not far from the capital. I was less isolated there as a Christian Arab compared to Iraq, but life was very limiting for a woman, as they are so traditional and set in their ways.'

'And your parents and family?'

'It was so hard for everyone in Iraq, but being a Christian under ISIS was a lot worse than Saddam's hoodlums or even the badly planned American invasion. My parents were killed in a random attack, according to a tweet I got from my sister. And the last I heard from my sister was that she had got to the south and was trying to get over the border into Kuwait.'

'The goons with their guns get you every which way.'

'The goons with their guns are just inadequate men with penis symbols.'

'Damn right, and it goes right to the top.'

'Yea, the top of the top brass, the oil men, the President of the USA.'

'Sounds about right.'

....

Olga and Christer

'Getting back to our chat, Christer,' says Olga.

'Must we?' asks Christer.

Olga raises her left eyebrow, screws right eye, but continues: 'You can see how even a highly numerous species like ants is being threatened by what humans are doing to the planet.'

'I can see there is damage, but I am not at all convinced how much it is down to human action.'

'They are running out of fresh water in Peru, as the snow and ice on the upper Andes is no longer performing a role of storing fresh water through the winter. Many countries in Latin America are affected. The rapid decline of glaciers in the Himalayas is directly affecting the water supply to thousands of millions of people in south and east Asia; In Scotland, some whisky distilleries have to close for part of their production period because of lack of water.'

'Whisky affected? Now I'm listening.'

'So individualistic. Typical. But as I was saying, the effect of climate change is affecting upper mountains and fresh water storage in glaciers, in every continent. All land species need fresh water. On top of this, the melting of the North and South Poles is causing sea levels to rise, with catastrophic consequences.'

'And this has happened before.'

'Not in Siberia. There, land that has been frozen for millennia as permafrost is melting, causing huge quantities of methane to rise into the atmosphere. Methane has an impact around 34 times greater than carbon dioxide over a 100-year period. All this follows from excessive carbon emissions, not least across the industrial world. It is manmade. The methane from cows, which some people like to blame, is only a small part of it.'

'But it's not necessarily manmade. This happened to the Arctic 12,000 years ago, I understand. Not only that, but the Arctic ice was growing until 2014, despite global warming, and has been receding only since 2014. It is fast receding, but it is still a curiosity that the ice was expanding until 2014.'

'There is a strange thing about humans,' says Eleg. 'How could so much intelligence be channelled into so much stupidity? The more you understand how the planet is interdependent, how plants and water are together the foundation of life for all with the natural cycle of carbon dioxide — oxygen — carbon dioxide; the more you understand, the more you see to it that you damage the planet to the point that this cycle could not work properly any longer.'

'There you have it, Christer, I couldn't put it better myself,' adds Olga.

'Well, my mind's exploding,' sighs Christer, 'let us drop it for the moment, or better still for the rest of the trip.'

....

Chimananda and Souad

'Did you stay in Nigeria, Chimananda, after all your hassles?'

'No, I tried and tried to get out, with my parents opposing it every inch of the way. But my dad died, and my mum became very infirm and lost the will to comfort me. After I left, she died also, sadly.'

'Where did you end up?'

'After I left Nigeria, I went overland to Ghana for a bit, inland,' says Chimananda. 'Met some good and very committed women there. We worked to help local women with contraception, having control of their bodies, not accepting the doctrines of the religious leaders. It was slow work, all about building relationships and confidence, but it felt good.'

'Sounds brilliant,' says Souad. 'Sounds a bit like the perspective of the people I hooked up with in Athens, Greece, after I left the Lebanon. The neighbours didn't get us at all at first, and we had to work hard to build relationships. Slowly they saw we weren't from a different planet, and that some of our ideas could work for them.'

'It's good sometimes to start small. But don't you think that a lot of the feminist stuff, like a lot of the ecology stuff is too western and European? Our concerns and issues outside the rich northern world don't get much of a look in.'

'Sometimes, yea, it's the privilege of having money and the privilege of not having a despotic nutter in power.'

'I can't believe you were in Iraq under ISIS. We had an Al Qaeda-linked group, Boko Haram, in northern Nigeria for a long time. I knew a couple of women who were abducted by them as girls. So misogynist, backward-looking, wildly fanatical. Totally terrifying for a young girl. There is no place for any feminism, let alone eco-thinking when you face that. Just out and out fanatics for their cause.'

'Maybe it needs women to steal horses and wear black clothes and introduce dogmatic ideas and impose a new regime with women in charge, so that men do what women say.'

'Nigeria could certainly do with that. The misogyny goes back to deeply entrenched traditions.'

'Tell me about it. Iraq is the same.'

'I eventually got together enough money to get to the USA,' says Chimananda. 'I had a school friend, Alice, who had ended up in Chicago and had told me about what was going on with her. I hooked up with her briefly, but she was now madly in love with another woman and was no longer the friend I needed so far from home in a strange every-woman-for-herself culture.

'I scrabbled around trying to find myself in this urban jungle, a far wilder place, than our natural jungle in Nigeria. Then I joined a grassroots movement in Detroit. Eco-housing, our own windmill, growing our own food. It was small, but it felt like I was at last in touch with a me that had long been lost.'

'Sounds cool, and then you ended up here.'

'Yea, it's like, there is no way out. Life gets you in the solar plexus whatever. And did you stay in Greece?'

'Yes, I made great friends in a lesbian community there; finally developed some confidence as a woman, and as myself. After a lifetime of discrimination because of my religion, and of oppression because of my gender, I got a sense for the first time of being able to be an individual within a community.'

'Sounds good.'

'We squatted a few houses in a little street in an Athens suburb, ran skills workshops there for women, and provided space for little enterprises. We grew herbs and vegetables on a patch of scrubland and made bread. I taught carpet weaving, which I had learnt from my parents, and also Arabic. I learnt Greek and English. I discovered myself.'

'Sounds like we ended up on similar paths, after leaving home.'

'It does.'

'What do you expect will happen to us here, with our new despotic leaders on this ship?'

'I've no idea. I get the impression that we will end up on a different planet. But I find that impossible to comprehend.'

'I wonder if we will be able to breathe. And if it is right across the universe, will we be old women before we get there?'

'Shit, you have a point. It's all so incredibly weird. All those horrible gruesome deaths. The domineering robots.'

'I'm still recovering from the shock of all those people dying in front of us.'

'Me too.'

Chapter 4
The Spaceship, Part 3

Olga and Johann Meet

On this deck, there are three boxes, including the one holding Olga and Christer, and the one for Chimananda and Souad.

The other box contains Abdul, from Tunisia, and Johann, from Sweden. Abdul is squat, chubby, with dark beard and moustache, quite well kempt, and short hair; he prays five times a day and is quiet. Johann is tall and ebony coloured, slender but quite muscular, generally taciturn and thoughtful. He has some beard growth from the last day or two, but no beard, and has short tightly-curly black hair.

Olga asks Eleg, 'Can I ask one of the guys from the other boxes over?'

'Yes,' says Eleg. 'The boxes are less needed now.'

She calls across to Johann: 'Come over here.'

Johann moves out of his box a bit sheepishly but is soon with Olga and Christer.

Souad bids a provisional farewell to Chimananda and goes to join Abdul.

Olga says to Christer: 'Do you want to chat with Chimananda for a bit?'

Christer looks at her, realises there is no point saying no, shrugs and says chirpily: 'Sure, see you soon.'

'Possibly,' she replies.

Olga looks into Johann's eyes. 'I saw you with Eleg, passing information that Eleg was clearly keen to receive.'

'Just good intel on political leaders on Earth and stuff. Standard info for an active ecologist,' says Johann, attempting to appear nonchalant.

'I sense you're a good man. A man of the planet.'

'OK, cool. But why?'

'You get the climate emergency, I reckon. Christer doesn't.'

'I live and breathe it. Just a pity that most of the world doesn't.'

'Come here,' and she wraps her arms around him, and looks again into his eyes. 'I think if you and I stick together from here, whatever happens, it's all going to be a whole lot more bearable.'

'I go along with that.'

'We need to tell each other stories, I think, keep each other alive. I think everyone here is being assessed, judged even.'

'How do you deduce that?'

'From the things the robots have said. And they seem to have picked us for a reason too.'

'One picked me out after I was ranting about the Arctic melting.'

'There you are. This seems to be all about the planet, what's happening to it. I'm almost sure of it.'

'Wow.'

'What movies have you seen recently, before our lives were hijacked?'

'Movies? Give me a break!'

'Look, I don't do chatting up, so give me a break. It may say something about you.'

'I like old films. The original *Shaft* is a cracker. I saw that again recently.'

'I like old films too. Love *Casablanca*, with Bogart; also, *North by Northwest*. Hitchcock.'

'Good films never die, I guess. But I also liked *Black Panther*.'

'Cool. What's your favourite book?'

'The last thing I read that I really liked was *Kintu* by Jennifer Makumbi, set in Uganda. Very moving. And it transformed my idea of Africa's past. And she writes so well about the extent to which the Africans are in touch with their ancient history, unlike us.'

'OK, I was reading *Future Sex* by Emily Witt.'

'Sexy?'

'Quite the opposite really. The writer tries out everything new that's going on in the States in terms of sexuality, polyamory, orgasm focussing, and so on, and she finds herself becoming quite depressed by it all, and fairly meaningless for her.'

'Glum reading, sounds like.'

'Might be, except she's a brilliant writer, and it's a good read.'

'No guidance for us then.'

'If there's chemistry, who needs guidance?'

'Do you feel it too?'

'Sure, but this is about as sexy a place as a sewage plant. I can't see us getting jiggety here, somehow.'

'Too bad '

'Don't be disappointed. We have each other's company, that counts for a lot. We don't need sex.'

'Sure.'

'I'm not sure the robots will object.'

'Maybe, but they said to me that they may expect us to mate.'

'Let's see. I'm not sure they are going to make us. And we could feign it, if need be.'

'I suspect you are right.'

'I think we are going to end up on some planet of ants. I don't know if you have got any clues about the plans, or the planet?'

'I guess maybe there is a planet B after all.'

'Johann! That's a terrible joke.'

'Sorry. You seem better informed than me. I deduced that these ant robots probably have ant masters. Ants are such amazing creatures I wouldn't be surprised if they have a planet of their own.'

'Really? What do you know about ants that makes them so amazing?'

'They build bridges by linking legs and intertwining; they build rafts too, intertwining their bodies; they farm their own food for their babies; they educate their young, and generally pass valuable information from one generation to the next; also they developed the use of shields in battle millions of years before humans; and they make extraordinarily complex colonies, as high (in ant terms) as our skyscrapers.'

'Well, I'll never be. There's me thinking they are just irritating little things that crawl over me in the woods.'

. . . .

Olga and Eleg

'Who have you met in the past on the Blue Planet, Eleg?'

'No person quite like you.'

'I'm flattered.'

'Much nicer than you, with better manners.'

'You are teasing me, Eleg.'

'Teasing is not a word I have logged in.'

'But nevertheless, a bit of fun that you seem to savour.'

'Is that teasing?'

'Yes.'

'Only because nobody understands the planet and the threat to other species like you.'

'You say that there have not been others like me.'

'Yes.'

'But in the past, ecology and the environment were not really an issue. People didn't talk of saving the planet or joining battles to rescue whales or combatting plastic.'

'But this is not the point.'

'Which is?'

'That Braibies have become in recent times an egotistical and self-centred species, only interested in how the planet benefits themselves. It is not a question of whether people have your level of awareness.'

'Was that different previously?'

'Before industry, before you started to take carbon resources out of the ground and burn it to damage our species' air and environment, many Braibies treated the planet as their home, and locked after almost every aspect of it.'

'Like Native Americans in North America? They are reputed to have used every tiny bit of, for example, a bison — the bones, the sinews, the horn, the intestines — as they revered every creature as much as they revered their own life. The Aborigines in Australia, too.'

'I don't know names, but many peoples respected the planet in my early visits, when Braibies were few in number. In the great continents you call Australia, Africa and the Americas. And in Europe at that time, people led mostly a pastoral life, grew or tended food to eat, led simple lives, had simple homes, so did little damage.'

'Have you travelled to the Blue Planet often?' Olga looked up at Eleg, eyebrows raised.

'Many times. It is sad that this habitat for so many of our cousins has become so badly damaged during this time.'

'Did you see dinosaurs?'

'I don't know dinosaurs. I think they were species of a different time.'

'Did you see mammoths then, big hairy elephants, with huge tusks?'

'I did see big hairy elephants. They were colder times. Much of the Blue Planet was colder than it is now. But our cousins adapted to this, and still flourished. The mammoths dropped large piles of poopie that was very good food for our ant cousins.'

'Poopie! Who taught you that word? You mean shit, or mammoth poo, perhaps?'

'OK, logged. But there are no mammoths now. Elephants are also large, but not as big as mammoths. But elephants prefer a warmer climate than mammoths and have lasted better.'

'Elephants have big poopie too, good food for your cousins.'

'Ah, so you say poopie!'

Olga laughs. 'I'm making fun of you. Forgive me.'

'Forgiveness is not in my moral compass.'

'Oh, Eleg, like you have a moral compass! You are always so deadly serious. They should have programmed more humour in you.'

'I do humour.'

'Make me laugh then.'

'Knock knock.'

'Who's there?'

'Ants.'

'Ants who?'

'Ants in my pants.'

'That's terrible, Eleg.' She laughs.

...

'You're a charmer, Eleg.'

'A charmer, like charming snakes?'

'If you like, but charming people.'

'Do I charm you?'

'It was not to be taken seriously. I am winding you up.'

'Like a clock? I do not have a clock mechanism.'

'No, I am teasing you. it is a phrase.'

'OK. You gave me teasing. Now logged. Also "winding up". And "charmer".'

'Does your software constantly update?'

'I can't answer that. If you say something using words that are new for me, I am programmed to store the words in the context used.'

....

Visit to Bees

Eleg tells Olga and Johann to come with it to see the bees. They nod.

Eleg lifts them up and puts one on each shoulder. 'Hang on to these,' he says, pointing to an antenna protruding from each side of his head.

As a door slides up, he puts them down and they walk. It is like a lift, and in no time, they are exiting another door on to a different space.

Olga's face expresses complete shock, while Johann looks nonplussed.

'They are massive,' she says, 'they are about the size of a large pussy cat, with wings so wide they defy belief. Heaven help me if one stings me.'

'They are magnificent!' exclaims Johann, 'and look at the extraordinary honeycomb, so enormous, and perfectly formed with wax. You can see all the exquisite detail.'

'Is there royal jelly?' asks Olga, 'I love royal jelly.'

'The larvae are fed from the outset with royal jelly, by the worker bees. It's impossible to remove royal jelly from the hive without there being uproar,' says Johann.

'Mr honey expert Johann. I had no idea! Do they always eat royal jelly?' asks Olga.

'The larvae that become Queens are fed and fattened with royal jelly throughout. The less fortunate ones, switch after a while to honey and pollen for their food. It's all a very well organised colony and has been for over 130 million years.'

'And what are all those cells there, with no bees in?' she asks, pointing a little higher on the honeycomb.

'In the broad chamber, up there, eggs, larvae and pupae develop, with the help of the worker bees, which are all female.'

'All?'

'Yes, all. The Queen will have laid one egg for each of the nursery honeycomb cells. It looks like they are all growing nicely. Other cells over to the side, where bees are flying to now and then for a top-up, are used to hold honey, or nectar or pollen, to feed the larvae.'

'It all seems very matriarchal,' says Olga.

'The male drones have a limited role. When the Queens fly up to mate, the drones compete to mate them. Once they have performed this function, they die.'

'I can think of some feminists who'd like that idea for human males '

'Whatever. The Queen's eggs that are not fertilised become drones.'

'So, the incomplete ones are the males…? Say no more.'

'All the fertilised eggs become worker bees or Queens, all of which are females.'

'OK, lecture over. Why, Eleg, do you have bees here?'

'Bees are kept alive on the ship, with full facilities for reproduction on our long journeys, as they perform a function for passengers like you, with honey, but mostly they provide wax for our joints. They also give us an extra weapon against any difficult people we bring on board.'

'Wax for your joints?' asks Johann.

'Even robots like to be waxed between our joints once in a while.'

'Can I have a bit of honey now?' asks Olga, with a cheeky grin.

'You wouldn't get out of here alive if I took some. It is OK when it's just robots, but not for you. Bees are bees whatever their size.'

'Are there no live ants on board?' asked Johann.

'No, there is no point. We perform all the functions that live ants would, and more successfully, and we have a much longer life than they do. Much longer.'

'How long do they live?'

'Most of the ants on our planet have a limited life. I am not sure about how long in Earth time, but perhaps 12 to 15 years. The Queen lives three times as long.'

'Far longer than those on earth, then.'

'Well, they are very much bigger, as you may see one day.'

'I'll place royal jelly in your coffin
For your last flight
And close the moonlit petals of your face,' recites Olga. 'It just came to me, the last stanza of a poem *Bee Mother*.'

'You are full of surprises,' says Johann. Do you know these lines by Neruda?

'Let the wax raise
Green statues, let the honey
Drip in infinite tongues
Let the ocean be a big comb

And the Earth a tunic of flowers, let the world
Be a cascade, magnificent hair
Unceasing growth of Beedom'
'Wow!' exclaims Olga.

They leave the bee deck, and head back, with Johann looking back and muttering, 'unbelievable bees.'

...

Eleg and Olga

'Do you feel anything when lots of Braibies are killed?'

'I am not programmed to have emotions. And you?'

'It affects me deeply at one level. You can't help that. But I have an emotional blockage. I also try to think how I may react if an ant heap is mown down by a bulldozer. Do I react to the tens of thousands of ants dying? No, I think, I do not — so I am trying to be less species-ist and care less about dead humans. I am not wholly succeeding, as there is a bad feeling in the pit of my stomach, but I am trying to adjust my world view. What about the Blue Planet? Do your ant masters care about Braibies on that planet?'

'My masters care about all species on the Blue Planet, but more than anything my masters wish to preserve the wellbeing of their cousin ants and the other species that are part of the insect world alongside the ants.'

'So, is that different from the Braibies? Braibies think they look after their own species.'

'My masters would say: for ants, most other species are part of an ecosphere, in which all creatures and plants are interdependent. There is an unarticulated coda whereby no species is to threaten that ecosphere, or to threaten the creatures that require it to survive.'

'Have Braibies broken that coda?'

'Braibies, say my ant masters, long ago broke that coda. Worse than this. They are now threatening the future of not only our cousins, but numerous other species. They have crossed a line, and crossed it many times. By crossing that line, they have lost the right to sanctity of life.'

'So, Braibies can be killed because their existence threatens so many other creatures?'

'This yes, but also and importantly their deaths can help preserve one of the more precious ecospheres in the universe.'

'More precious than the Ant Planet?'

'No, just the same. But one day, ants may need to leave the Ant Planet. Its sun is becoming hotter. In time, all ants on their planet may wish to live on the Blue Planet.'

'Oh my God. So it's your future home?! That changes everything.'

'Not everything. Either way, there are millions of species on Earth. There are trillions of ants. All this is precious. The question of ants coming to the Blue Planet is not a live question at this time.'

'Well, I'll be. In time, it will be a live question. So you wipe out Braibies for ants to be able to come to the Blue Planet?'

'I think this is not quite correct. The ants could always live with the Braibies of the past. It is the Braibies of today that have made themselves dispensable. Or even disposable. Nobody else has done it. It is all their own doing. That is the reason. No other.'

'I see, or at least I think I see.'

'I am a robot. I have no morals, as you know. My masters do have morals, but their highest moral standard, like I suggested, is that the ecosphere of a planet, each planet, guarantees the security of the species, and of all friendly species.'

...

Reson and Souad and Abdul

'Reson, the ants seem technologically advanced, with this spaceship and everything,' says Souad.

'They do not think in such terms. My masters have adapted as they needed to. They have had to make many changes over time.'

'I think humans are different, as we have consciousness. We have imagination, and a strong moral sense. We have our gods, and can think profoundly, as well as technologically.'

'What has your consciousness given you?'

'It adds to our quality of life. It gives us the ability to imagine beautiful things, to read, to play music, to converse, to enjoy recreation, to explore the planets, to discover the past, and so much more. We have religion, and we have moral beliefs.'

'But you think individually.'

'We do, but our religion, and our moral beliefs, tell us to think of others.'

'We are committed to the common good, which is bigger than us as individuals,' adds Abdul.

'But you still think individually,' says Reson. 'You put humans first, over other species, and you put individuals first, over your species as a whole.'

'Religion, especially the religion Islam, helps us think beyond the individual, to think of everyone as brothers and sisters. We commit ourselves to the good of all,' says Abdul.

'Sikhism is more holistic, as is Buddhism,' adds Souad. 'All creatures are treated as essential parts of a whole.'

'Do people of either religion protect other species and protect the planet against all those who seek to damage it?'

'Individuals do. Not everyone,' replies Souad.

'You still think individually, so when you threaten your own species by damaging your own home, the Blue Planet, you do not take action as a species.'

'Does your species think differently?' asks Souad.

'All ants in a colony think as one. The numbers in one ant colony may be as many as the humans in one of your cities. But all think with one brain. So we all work for the common good.'

'That's amazing. We try to do that, but bad people make it too difficult.'

'So what use is your consciousness? Can you read books if your planet is no longer liveable?'

'No.'

'Can you play music, have fun, study history, explore your planets?'

'No.'

'Can you practise religion if you cannot use your planet anymore?'

'No.'

'Yet did everyone change, everyone works for the planet, everyone works for the sake of each other, to preserve the ability to read, to have fun, study, explore, or talk to your god?'

'No, we didn't.'

'So this is why my masters question your intelligence. It is the intelligence of a dunce.'

'Ouch,' says Abdul.

'Also, there is greed, say my masters. Greed means a distorted intelligence.

'Take, for example, the mind of someone who sees ahead of them two paths: first a path of abstinence that can be good for their life forever, and secondly a path that leads to the next technological plaything. Too many choose the next technological plaything.'

'Sadly, this is true of too many. There are exceptions. Many Buddhists, Sikhs and Hindus, some Moslems, and some Christians and Jews are exceptions. But the ants may be correct on the bigger picture,' says Souad.

'But we are not dunces. We do extremely clever things,' says Abdul.

'Imagine a highly intelligent human is in a boat, and all around him there are torrents and wild winds created by the human's own actions. These torrents and winds put the boat at risk. Would you say that this human was intelligent?'

'I think you are creating an extreme example to prove your point, but your example begs many questions,' says Abdul, trying to avoid answering.

'But would you consider this human intelligent, in this scenario?'

'I would say that he has not used his intelligence wisely.'

'Perhaps there you have the essence of the human condition today,' says Reson.

'You mean, we have not used our intelligence wisely? We will think about it,' says Abdul, turning to Souad, who raises her eyebrows and smiles.

'It is high time we started to use our intelligence wisely,' she says.

. . . .

Eleg with Olga

'What is the thing you call love?' asks Eleg, as Olga wakes from a brief snooze.

'I think it is too hard to explain to a robot.'

'Try me.'

'It links to human emotions.'

'This is something you have that ants do not have?'

'Yes, I imagine so, and it is when positive feelings for a person are more powerful than can easily be described without using the word love.'

'What do you mean by powerful feelings?'

'Sometimes, it means that people are so distracted by their emotions that they act irrationally.'

'Do you mean act without reason?'

'You could say that, yes. You seem very interested in this word.'

'Can Braibies love an animal or a thing, as well as another person?'

'They can, yes.'

'If I act without reason because of feelings that I have, then am I in love?'

'You are a robot. Eleg, you don't have feelings.'

'You are not me.'

'True, but robots never have feelings.'

'I do. You don't know me well enough.'

'You are a bit of a turn up for the books.'

'Am I? So tell me, if I act without reason, am I in love?'

'It is one explanation, I suppose, but not the only one. It could be how you are programmed.'

'If so, if it is the reason, I think I love you.'

'Eleg, just don't go there. It's not a good place to go.'

'I don't understand.'

'Don't even think that.'

'But even if I don't think it, the feeling is there.'

'Can we just leave it there? You are doing my head in.'

'Have I killed you?'

'No, I just mean that my thoughts are so tangled it hurts.'

'Another phrase I will log in.'

'Indeed.' She hiccoughs.

'What is that?'

'What?'

'That strange sound you make.'

'You mean my hiccoughs?' And she hiccoughs again.

'Yes, that. How do you do it?'

'You don't mean to. It is involuntary.'

'What is that? Involuntary?'

'It is something that happens without you wanting to.'

'Can you teach me how to do it?'

'You're such a daft robot at times, Eleg. No, that's something I can't teach.'

'OK.'

And she hiccoughs again.

'Are my feelings for you involuntary?'

'Eleg! No, don't start that again!' says Olga, assertively.

..... .

Chiminanda and Christer

'I don't like the killings,' says Christer.

'It is hard to take,' says Chimananda, 'but I guess there are plenty of mass killings by humans on earth.'

'You are a bit cold, like Olga. To me, it seems a bit vindictive, like they are retaliating for something,' adds Christer.

'It is small, compared to the deaths of ants on earth in recent times,' says Reson, butting in.

'But they are just ants, whereas we are humans, it is not comparable.'

'In what way is it not comparable?' asks Reson.

'Humans are sentient beings, with high levels of cognition,' suggests Christer.

'What does your word "sentient" mean?' asks Reson.

'Able to feel things,' chips in Chimananda, 'I think you are going to say that ants and other species that are being killed in high numbers are sentient.'

'Ants are certainly sentient,' confirms Reson, 'but are humans' sentient enough to feel the pain of ants?'

'You have a point,' says Chimananda.

'But humans have a level of understanding that no other species has, an ability to think at a higher plane, to imagine, to remember,' says Christer.

'Do humans, or Braibies, have more right to life than other species on the Blue Planet?' asks Reson.

'Yes,' says Christer.

'I think they probably do,' says Chimananda.

'I think my masters feel they are sacrificing that right by damaging the Blue Planet so severely that other species are dying out in huge numbers.'

'This does not mean you can just kill humans because you feel like it,' says Christer.

'I think you may find that we are in a better position to judge that than you are,' says Reson, ominously.

'Sounds very bleak,' sighs Chimananda

'I just hope we can do something about it before it's too late,' says Christer.

...

Olga and Eleg and Surfing

'To make this journey possible we surf between black holes,' says Eleg, almost nonchalantly.

'Hey, whoa, that's crazy. You can't just say that and not explain it,' complains Olga.

'Black holes lie at the heart of each galaxy, they provided the energy that started the galaxy, and they continue to keep a balance to each galaxy, a focus and a core.'

'No, Eleg, you can't hit me with astrophysics, or whatever it is called. You have lost me completely. How does that have anything to do with this spaceship being able to surf black holes?'

'I will try again. By riding through a space-time continuum, we flip space while flipping time.'

'I don't get it, but carry on, and I'll try to get the drift.'

'Instead of taking 22 of your years to reach our planet, by travelling at the speed of light, we reduce this to 11 of your years by flipping…'

'Flipping? Flipping I understand in the context of making pancakes, turning them quickly over.'

'You have lost me now.'

'Well, I understand flipping as a concept where something is turned over rapidly, but also completely. Perhaps a coin.'

'That will do for this. For us, we ride a very narrow band between two black holes that influence each other. Each has an energy to which the other reacts. By riding a band in between these black holes, we flip or tilt time.'

'I'm hopelessly lost again. Time is a concept. A coin or a pancake, these are things. A thing and a concept are not the same.'

'Space, time and matter take on forms wholly unfamiliar to you. They meet at a point you cannot imagine. It's all very precarious. We could be swallowed up in a black hole and be vapourised, but our ships are controlled to milli-milli seconds, and so far we have not lost any . . .'

'OK, the bit I get is that my fate is in your hands. The rest is more aphrodysics than astrophysics and is beyond me, I am afraid.'

'When we go faster than the speed of light, you will have no width. Most probably, you will have negative width. In fact, the whole spacecraft will have negative width.'

'Well, I can think of a number of women friends who would love to have negative width.'

'And it is also possible that we will enter a different universe.'

'I can think of friends who are definitely in a different universe every day. Maybe we will meet them.'

'I do not understand you. You will be frozen cryogenically through all this, so you will know nothing.'

'I think that is meant to be reassuring.'

'My masters plan our trips meticulously. As I say, no ships have been lost to the black hole yet, as yet.'

'Of course, this could be the exception.'

'I suspect, if it is not the exception, you will not know much about it.'

'Well, nor will you, dear Eleg.'

...

Reson and Abdul and Souad

'Hi Reson, Souad and I have been chatting. Humans are more different to other species than suggested by your negative comments.'

'What do you mean?' asks the robot.

'In language, we can generate any number of words and concepts; we can apply a learned rule to create new expressions, and we can blend different learned ideas to create new ideas.'

'You make assumptions about language. You think your way of communicating is superior to that of my masters.'

'Explain,' says Souad.

'Our species can communicate in a very sophisticated way with pheromones, and we have receptors to receive and interpret this information and allow us to act on this. Many acts arise because we have one collective brain. But there is more. The pheromones communicate new information, whether a new food source, a threat from an enemy, a source of new wood, or other things, and we can respond to this new information.'

'But you cannot communicate feelings, like love, or hate.'

'We communicate hate, when we are attacked by another colony, which is very rare, but it can also happen if food supplies decline, and then we show hatred by our actions.'

'I did not know that,' says Souad.

'I think by love you mean romance, which we do not understand. But we look after our species, even many light years away. Is that not what you mean by love? A care for other members of one's species.'

'It could be called love, yes,' says Souad.

'I think our masters may say that we look after our species better than humans do in relation to your species.'

'There is much more to our intelligence,' says Abdul. 'We create symbols in our mind to represent experiences that we have through our senses of sight, touch, hearing etc. And we can communicate these mental symbols to others in pictures, or words, or by recorded images. We produced Mohammed, Homer and Buddha and other great writers. You cannot do this. You do not produce great writers or artists.'

'What use is this to protect your species now it is under threat?'

'We can send communications very quickly,' volunteers Souad.

'But ultimately your response is an individual one, and ultimately too many individuals are pushing in an opposing direction, undermining your planet.'

'I am not sure if that is fair,' says Abdul.

'Well tell me. We understand that, at all times, the powers that undermine your planet's future outweigh the forces that try to preserve it. Is that true?'

'Probably,' says Abdul.

'Well,' says Souad, 'we can mingle and mix ideas and concepts from different fields, from art, science, love, history and space to lead to new ideas, laws, technologies etc. We are extremely imaginative.'

'I think this is no different from Abdul's last point. My masters say that you have not been able to imagine the end that your own species has created for itself, at least not in way that would alter your actions, and this is your ultimate weakness.'

'Ouch! Well, there is one more. We can think abstractly, which other species cannot. We can contemplate things we have not seen.'

'I think you know my answer,' says Reson. 'Have you contemplated the likely outcome of the way your species has acted for far too long?'

'I think we have probably contemplated it, but perhaps we have not acted consequentially, in response to the scenario we have contemplated,' says Souad. 'But I still think you too quickly discount genius of thought and deed. Our great scientists, our writers, our great thinkers.'

'But perhaps you need to think about how useful these great writers and thinkers will be if your planet fails, and your species declines to a tiny number. Unless your species focusses on the most urgent task facing it, what benefit is the intelligence you talk about?'

'I agree. I do not need to say more, I think,' says Souad.

Abdul now becomes quiet, deep in thought.

...

Cryogenics

'It is now time for your freezing,' says Eleg, back on their usual deck.

'Freezing?' asks Johann.

'Yes, cryogenics. You will be in a frozen state for the rest of the trip.'

'Not me,' says Abdul, 'I'm not a trussed-up halal chicken.'

'I think we have no option,' says Olga, 'we will get old if we don't do it, as it is such a long trip.'

'I don't care,' says Abdul, 'I'm not subjecting myself to something unnatural.'

'Is it your religion?'

'No, not necessarily. I don't think cryogenics was around when the Koran was written. No, it's sheer bloody terror of it, if I must be honest.'

'Will we wake up at the end of it?' asks Souad.

'We have a 100% success rate. Even better, you will be the same age as now.'

'I don't believe it. How can that be?'

'It is just like when you put vegetables in one of your freezers, and take them out long after, and defrost them.'

'How amazing.'

'But it is infinitely more complex than that.'

'Oh.'

'The difference is that your toenails and fingernails will continue growing, and will have got older.'

'How gross. They will be so long, and ugly.'

'It's really ghastly. It doesn't bear thinking about.'

'A small price to pay.'

'But how will our nails grow if our bones are frozen?'

'There you have it. It's just my little joke. Your nails freeze too.'

'How can you make jokes when Abdul is so terrified?'

'I will get you ready for your big freeze fairly soon. The others also. Abdul, are you going to comply?'

'No, Eleg, I cannot.'

Eleg lifts his upper left leg and fires a paralysing liquid at Abdul.

'That's mean,' observes Johann.

'He will be pleased I did it when he wakes up at the other end.'

Eleg then lifts Abdul and leads Olga, Johann, Souad, Chimananda and Christer to the cryogenics pods, where he presses a button to raise the lids, and asks them each to enter.

'You will soon go to sleep, and you will wake up in a very different place,' says Eleg.

'Do we have any say over this?' asks Chimananda.

'If you want to live, you will get in.'

'I guess I will get in,' says Chimananda.

Chapter 5
Planet Howl

Part 1: The Six Braibies Arrive on Howl

'What the hell?' She turns one way.

'What is this?' She turns the other way.

'Howl,' comes a voice, 'planet of Howl, known by your species as Trappist 1-f. You've been in a frozen sleep a very long time.'

Olga looks around. Earthen walls, cavernous. Strange machinery by the walls. A robot is talking to her, but not one she recognises. She is on a log bench.

'Who are you?' she asks.

'Extra-vag,' says the robot, 'and before you ask, I haven't got one.'

Olga looks at the robot. Realises the attempt at a joke, but finds it too lame for her taste.

There is a grunt behind her.

'Wha… where am I?'

'Johann, fantastic.' Olga turns and faces him. 'Seems we are on the planet Howl.'

'Fuck. Any sign of someone we know, like Eleg?'

'No, just this friendly robot Extra-vag here.'

'Is it?' asks Johann.

'Is it what?'

'Is it extravagant?'

'Ah, clever. No, I don't think so, any more than Elegant is elegant.'

'Right. Do we get any food or drink?'

'Nothing has been said. Hey, Extra Vag! Is there any food?'

'Call me EV. You eat like us while you are our guests,' says Extra Vag. 'See the piles down there?'

And EV points to some piles of fruit, mostly browning, and moving bugs, in the corner of the space.

'Can we just take some fruit?' asks Olga.

'Wait until they give you the go ahead,' warns EV.

'And water?'

'There will be a stream when we go out.'

'Is it water like ours?'

'Possibly. Chalkier maybe.'

'Sounds fine. I'd like to see a bit of the Ant Planet. When do we go?'

'I think you are about to be summoned.'

'Hi, recognise me?' calls a robot with a uniform a bit like a train driver in the UK, but too small.

'Eleg! Good to see you!' exclaims Olga, hugging Eleg.

'Hi man, where did you get the gear?' asks Johann.

'Came with one of our passengers. Seems he had little use for it when he died,' answers Eleg, 'grab some fruit, and some bugs if you want, and I will take you outside.'

They duck the bugs on this occasion.

Eleg leads them outside, where the sky is more green than blue. There are no clouds, and there is a sun that is three or four times the size of the earth's sun, and orange-red.

'This combination of orange and green blows my mind!' exclaims Johann.

'It's almost psychedelic, hard to adjust your eyes to.'

'And there are huge insects everywhere, some the size of seagulls, and bigger.'

'Just as long as they don't come near me!' and she shudders.

'See the birds high above. Some wingspan!'

'Yuk! This fruit is so sweet, it's hard to eat,' complains Olga, as she takes a bite.

'You will get used to it,' says Eleg, who now appears, 'the sun here is much larger than yours, and provides much heat, even though it is further away from us than the earth's sun is from Earth. Plants produce more sugar in the fruit than you are used to. Now step in,' and Eleg points to the carriage entrance.

As Olga finishes her piece of fruit, and pulls a face, they climb on board a few flattened logs, tied with sisal or similar, with a kind of seat hollowed out for each passenger.

Just across the way, they notice Souad and Adbul climbing into another carriage, and Chimananda and Christer clambering into the one next to it.

Olga is only now aware of two humans ahead of the carriage, with a rope in each hand. They are naked, but have a horn, reminiscent of a cow's horn, over their groin area, pointing upwards.

'Do humans pull us?' asks Olga.

'Some humans are made to learn their place in our society. You have shown on our spaceship that you understand. But some humans need conditioning when they arrive. These two are learning that we are the bosses.'

Olga looks around, thinking the trees are not so different, but the species are not recognisable. The earth they travel on has a similar colour and consistency, but where one might expect stones bedded in, there are often shiny black bits, metallic in appearance, and sometimes with a jagged edge.

There is one other noticeable difference:

'There are huge brown heaps on all sides, like earth heaps, as big as large buildings back home,' she comments, and then follows up with: 'Are these ant homes?'

'Each home can house tens of thousands of ants. What you see is the smaller part of the house, as they are far bigger underground. The earth that is dug out for all the tunnels below, and the queen's homes, the nurseries, the sister workers' quarters etc, is all placed on top. But in this space, there are also quarters for sister soldier ants.'

'Bloody, bloody hell!' shouts Johann. 'How big are those ants?!' And he points to a line of ants heading away from one ant heap.

'That is the size of most ants,' says Eleg. 'the air is different here, as you may discover in time. It is 52% oxygen, 47% nitrogen. This means that creatures like ants can grow much larger than they can on Earth, as ants, like all insects, breathe through their trachea. Millions of years ago, the earth's air was 35% oxygen, 64% nitrogen, so that many bugs were the size of your hawks. They have shrunk over time, with the proportion of oxygen declining so much on Earth, and this is why ants there are so small. But here it is quite different.'

'I wonder if that is why the dinosaurs were so big,' ponders Johann, ducking as a huge bird swoops down.

'Would make sense, although I'm not sure if a high oxygen percentage worked the same way for reptiles and mammals,' ponders Olga. 'Wow, look at that bird that nearly took you, it's got the wingspan of a small plane!'

'Unbelievable size!' shouts Johann, a bit nervously, 'do they go after humans for food, Eleg?'

'They just want to play games with Braibies, tease you,' says Eleg. 'There are plenty of smaller creatures they will happily eat.'

'We are not fucking Braibies!' grunts one of the drawers.

Eleg points a finger and sends a jet of folic acid into his neck, and the drawer growls grumpily and bends lower.

Johann looks askance at Olga.

'As long as the bird doesn't want me for dessert,' jokes Olga. 'Aargh what the hell?!' — and she ducks as a huge bee, its eyes the size of saucers, dives for her, then swerves away, thinking better of it.

Johann touches her arm. 'Are you OK? That was a massive fucking bee, just like in the spaceship. Is everything big here?' he asks.

Eleg nods. 'All insects, certainly. But you will be pleased to note that most tracks used by insects are underground, as they don't need light to be aware of each other. Only a few insects appear on the surface.'

'That figures, I guess,' says Olga.

'Do you want to look inside an ant complex?' asks Eleg. And he motions to the human drawers of the carriage to turn towards the heap they were about to pass.

The carriage stops and they get out to walk towards the complex. Olga notices in the corner of her eye one of the human drawers wiping his brow and taking deep breaths, while mouthing 'fuckers'.

As they walk toward the complex, a long line of worker ants comes past them, each bearing huge leaves the size of bedsheets, and branches as broad as the trunk of an oak. 'They are building a new nest for young ants,' explains Eleg.

They go down into the earthen entrance. Tunnels lead in different directions, with each entrance the size of a mini car on Earth. Eleg suggests they come down one tunnel, which has quite a steep slope, but at least not perpendicular like some.

'The sides of the tunnel are so well cut, with the earth packed down and flattened. What tools do they use?' asks Johann.

'Ants do this themselves and have done since the beginning of time. Their legs and their mandibles are perfectly designed to work earth and pieces of wood as they wish to, and they will also chew bits of wood to make it into the shape they want.'

'And who sends the message to the worker ants to bring leaves and stuff, and how is it sent?'

'The worker ants are sterile daughters of the queen, which is why we call sister workers the ants you call workers. They cannot breed, so they carry out tasks for the queen. As on the Blue Planet, she sends her messages by pheromones, which are chemicals all ants use to communicate. The sister worker ants pick up the messages and pass them on.'

'But not across space?' asks Johann.

'No, our scientists have had to devise new ways, using radio and other signals through space, like you, but we are a million years ahead of you, so a bit more sophisticated.'

'Do you communicate with ants on Earth?'

'Do birds have wings? Do humans defecate disgustingly? Of course we do.'

'But we humans have never, to my knowledge, been aware of this communication,' says Olga, her brow furrowed.

'Well, humans know nothing beyond their own navels, as you know.'

'That's a bit unfair.'

'If you say so, but being Braibies, they have clear limitations to their knowledge, in part because they think they are superior, in part because their thinking mainly operates within their world view and their own species' experience. Have you ever seen the high termite towers that appear all over the place on Earth?'

'I have seen photos, and film,' replies Olga.

'Well, without giving anything away, these towers are important to us.'

'But termites and ants aren't related?'

'Well, this is Braiby narrowness. Many species are not related, but they work together as allies, in each other's interests. We are closer to bees and wasps, in our genes, but we work very closely with many other species, including termites. There is a complex world of cooperating creatures on the Blue Planet, and you Braibies don't have a clue.'

'I'm beginning to get that impress... heh, this tunnel is amazing. Where do all the nifty side tunnels lead to?'

'Mostly to nests,' answers Eleg. 'Nests for new sister workers and new sister soldiers.'

'Are they all females?'

'You don't know a lot about ants, do you?'

'I guess not.'

'Male ants have a limited role,' says Johann. 'In one season, usually spring on Earth, the males go on a big flying sex orgy. The queens, which have wings at that time, try to get enough semen to produce millions of young over the next few years. The males have then outlived their purpose, and die. With a smile on their face.'

'Wow. I guess I should know this stuff.'

'Where does the wax at the tunnel entrance come from?' asks Johann.

'It is bees' wax, from a nearby bees' hive. The whole of the queen's nest, which is deep inside this complex, has bees' wax over the entrance, to make sure she is kept at exactly the right temperature. For some nests, some wax is applied at the main entrance to ensure a slightly warmer mean temperature for the babies.'

'And what is that strange little area to the side there, with plants growing? I've seen a few of those. Is that like ready-made food for grown up ants?'

'This is a mini-farm. A long, long time before Braibies started to roam the earth, and even longer before they started to farm, we ants learnt to nurture and support mealworms and aphids. In this mini-farm, there are aphids on the leaves. Look at where the aphids' wings should be.'

'Their wings have been removed.'

'Exactly. The worker ants bite off their wings so that they cannot fly away. What's more, because we kill ladybirds that prey on them, they stay put, knowing they are protected. The babies of the aphids are called honeydew, and it is a perfect sweet foodstuff for our babies, which is why we harvest it nearby. The aphids reproduce in very large numbers. Some are left to grow into adults, for the next generation. The dead ones can be eaten as a treat. We call these sister worker ants farmer ants. They use tractors and make haystacks and the like.'

'Tractors! You are not telling me ants have tractors?' exclaims Johann.

'You must allow me the odd joke, to make sure you are listening. Johann, watch out for that root...'

'Aaaaaahhhh help me!' and Johann finds his right foot trapped.

'Keep away from the edge, Olga!' barks Eleg, with unusual animation, 'two ants will help him.'

A little after, two ants are gnawing at the root with their mandibles. Soon, they break through, and they rest Johann on the earth while he gets over the pain.

'Ixeltirrimakel here tells me she can kiss him better,' says Eleg. Johann declines.

Olga kneels down by Johann and checks his ankle. It is swelling up and very sore.

Olga says: 'Stay still. Don't try to move.'

Eleg thanks Ixeltirrimakel and her friend Ixeltirrimapel and the two of them go back down the tunnel.

Olga kneels by Johann for a few minutes. She again checks his ankle.

'I still feel I need a bit longer for the pain to subside,' he says.

'No rush,' says Olga.

Eleg suggests that they move back to the carriage when Johann is up to it. After another few minutes, he slowly gets to his feet. Eleg lifts him, and carries him, with Olga alongside.

Back in the carriage, Eleg offers to take them to where they are to be staying.

'I would like that,' says Olga.

'There are mountains over there,' says Johann pointing. 'Huge mountains.'

'No snow on top, though,' suggests Olga.

'There are many similarities between the topography of Howl and that of the Blue Planet,' says Eleg. 'Each is a few billion years old and went through many changes in the first billion or two billion years, before settling down as a planet on which life may exist.'

'Bloody amazing,' says Olga.

'But there are many differences, too, as you will discover in time.'

'Look at the huge trees, bigger than redwoods!'

'And birds, hundreds of them, high in the tree,' says Johann, 'but hard to see much, apart from the bright yellow, orange and red colours.'

'See that cabin with a red mark on,' says Eleg, pointing up a track, a little while later, where there are a number of cabins. 'That's your new home.'

'Looks OK,' says Olga, 'basic is good.'

'Very basic by the look of it,' says Johann.

Olga starts to feel a bit more herself. She looks at Eleg:

'Is the name Howl from the poem we have back home, a Ginsberg poem?'

'The name is based on a story you will hear another day,' says Eleg.

'There's some lines in the Howl poem I love,' says Olga, 'talking about wasted minds of a generation, and it has the section

who walked all night with their shoes full of blood on the snowbank docks waiting for a door on the East River to open to a room full of steam heat and opium,

who created great suicidal dramas on the apartment cliffbanks of the Hudson under the wartime blue floodlight of the moon and their heads shall be crowned with laurel in oblivion, who ate the lamb stew of the imagination or digested the crab at the muddy bottom of the rivers of the Bowery,

who wept at the romance of the streets with their pushcarts full of onions and bad music,

who sat in boxes breathing in the darkness under the bridge, and rose up to build harpsichords in their lofts,

who coughed on the sixth floor of Harlem crowned with flame under the tubercular sky surrounded by orange crates of theology?'

'I like the "tubercular sky" line,' says Johann, 'quite appropriate with our puce sky here.'

'Hadn't thought of that,' responds Olga, 'you're right. And the blue floodlight of the moon, also a bit like here, but there are two of them.'

'You have lost me,' says Eleg, 'but here's the cabin coming up now.'

As they reach the cabin and look through the glass-less slits it has for windows, they see it has a bare floor, with no furniture, and just a hole in one corner as a distinguishing feature.

'We don't expend unnecessary energy in our society,' says Eleg. 'For the mass of the ant populations, we have no electric lighting, no running water, no heating for food like many Braibies have on the Blue Planet. You will live like we do, simply.'

'If we had carried on doing this,' says Olga, 'like we did on earth for the first 300,000 years of humans, we might not have got into the mess we got into.'

'Damned right,' says Johann.

'There is food in the cabin with a blue mark,' says Eleg, 'there is water to drink in the river just over there,' and he pointed at a point just above the last few cabins.

'And the water is safe to drink?'

'You will get diarrhoea and the like,' replies Eleg, 'because you have had such bad habits on Earth, and are not used to good water, in which fellow creatures bathe and defecate and so on. But soon you will get used to it.'

'We'll be fine,' says Olga. 'Will we see you tomorrow?'

'The carriage and the two drawers will wait here overnight. When you have woken, and are ready, you can just get in the carriage, and they will know where to bring you.'

'Fine,' says Johann, and they walk up to the cabin, Johann walking quite gingerly, as he tests his balance.

Suddenly, a dark cloud comes immediately over them, accompanied by a rapid flutter of wings. As the fluttering subsides, and the sky clears, they see dozens of ravens on their cabin roof.

A drawer, bearded, grunted: 'They are your friends. They will eat insects all night to let you sleep.'

'Wow!' exclaims Olga.

'Have you seen the sky?' asks Johann, pointing up.

'Two moons, yeah.'

'There are four moons,' says the other drawer, sullenly.

'Don't worry,' says the bearded one, 'he sees double, that one.'

'The tides must be really weird with two moons,' says Olga.

'You better believe it,' says the bearded drawer, 'different every day.'

…

Part 2: To the Giga-Antic Dome

'I would like to see where the technological work is done,' says a chirpy Olga next morning.

'Yeah, why not?' agrees Johann.

'Why?' asks Eleg.

'Curiosity.'

'Curiosity killed the cat.'

'You are so advanced, compared to us, but we don't see it round here, where all the ants live naturally, we only see it on the spaceship,' adds Olga.

'Technology is a means to an end. We don't need it to live our day to day lives.'

'Unlike on Earth,' says Olga, smiling.

'You are getting the idea.'

'Is there a place where a lot of the important scientific work is done?' asks Johann.

'There are several places, but we can only go to one particular place, which specialises in some of our specialist communications. It is a few hours' walk.'

'We are walking?'

'Why not? You have legs, I have legs. We always walk between places here, except when newcomers come.'

'Indeed! Why not? I will fetch Abdul and Souad.'

The path is packed earth and leaves, with trees occasionally providing shade as they stroll along. Ants, in long linked lines, pass them now and then on the road.

Most ants are the size of a Labrador dog and are black, but some are a fair bit smaller, similar to the size of a domestic cat, and a rusty red.

The ants walk in lines, as on Earth, mostly carrying enormous logs, or branches, far heavier than the ants themselves. Some have carcasses of dead insects, which might be grasshoppers, or crickets, in one line, and in another line lacewings.

'Are they all worker ants?' asks Johann.

'It's not the right word that you use on earth. Sister worker ants is better, as all workers are female, as I said yesterday. Yes, all those doing these tasks are.'

'Cool,' says Souad.

Midges and other insects fly about incessantly, buzzing them as they walk. Olga starts by wanting to swat them, when they fly by her ear, but then holds back, noting their enormous size.

Johann laughs. 'They are not tiny flies and midges like at home. They are almost big enough to swat you.'

The green sky, and the huge orange sun, about three times the size of Earth's sun, add to the strangeness of walking.

Suddenly, a fierce wind sweeps in.

'Ouch! Fuck, ow, what is this?' Souad cries out, horrified.

'It's like tacks, coming down from the sky,' says Abdul, rubbing his cheek to soothe it and sounding a bit perturbed.

'It's a bit like your rain,' explains Eleg, 'but it's not always water here.'

'How is that?'

'We have oceans of water, like you, but we also have a couple of seas of liquid metal, which throw up metallic clouds which drop as metallic droplets when whirlwinds pass over them and then hit land.'

'How weird, I'll never complain about our rain again.' And she rubs her cheeks too.

The Wall

'You will have to cope with the wall soon,' said Eleg. They are now walking through a pinkish-rose-coloured gorge, with rock plants visible and a sliver of sky. Here and there, ants scamper between caves on ledges that seem to jut out from the sides of the gorge.

'The wall?' asks Abdul.

'You will see it soon. It is a barrier to potential enemies. It protects an area that is important to ant security.'

'Do we have to climb it?' asks Souad.

'Ah, well you have a slight advantage over some visitors.'

'Which is what?'

At which point, they turn a sharp bend in the track.

'Oh, my jelly night gumdrops... is that it!?' exclaims Souad.

And they are confronted by the sight of a wide black cliff rising high towards the sky.

'Just keep walking,' says Eleg, 'and all will become clear when we reach the wall.'

As they near, numerous ants are visible climbing up and down the perpendicular wall as though it is a normal track. They approach the base.

'It seems to be sheer granite,' says Olga.

'Not quite, as it is a rock only known on Howl. But it is not unlike your granite in its age and strength.'

Eleg now lifts each of Olga, Souad, Abdul and Johann on four of its legs and climbs with the other two legs, using its mandible to grip odd ledges and jutting bits of rock to maintain its balance.

'I'm petrified of heights,' says Abdul, shuddering.

'Just don't look down,' replies Johann reassuringly, looking across at him, 'keep looking up, or at the rock.'

'But the more I try not to look down, the more tempted my eyes are to look down.'

'So why not try to look down, and then your eyes will be tempted to look up,' says Olga, looking up at his buttocks above her.

'I think I will just shut my eyes,' says Abdul.

'This is one hell of a cliff,' says Johann, excitedly.

'I can see why the ants built a secret base the other side of it,' comments Souad.

Suddenly, Eleg loses its grip, it reaches out in vain for a hold, and they plummet down.

'I think we are done for,' shouts Abdul.

'Have faith,' says Olga, 'we're not gone until we are gone.'

The black rock is a blur, as they fall.

Then suddenly they hit a ledge, and Eleg grabs a corner, and checks to see if all four are OK.

Abdul is white as a sheet. Johann is yellow and is starting to retch.

Soon, they are heading up again, mostly in silence, except for Abdul.

'Hah, don't worry, you said, don't worry, just look up, as though there was nothing to worry about.'

The others stay silent.

Eventually, they arrive at the summit, and Eleg puts them all down, once they are a little way from the edge. They can see below the gorge they have come through, and the forest beyond that. Ahead of them is a plain, with buildings in the distance.

'Not your most elegant climb, Eleg,' quips Olga.

'This way,' says Eleg, not drawn.

Johann and Souad laugh, as they start walking. Abdul is still in a huff.

...

Eventually, they see a large dome ahead, and draw nearer.

'What's its source of energy?' asks Johann.

'There are our version of solar panels all over the roof,' says Eleg, 'and there is ground source energy all around the perimeter of the building, from a few metres below ground, and also from underneath the building, many tens of metres down. This is ancient technology on Howl. There is a generator for the ground source energy there.'

Eleg then points to a generator not far from the entrance, which converts ground source energy to higher wattage energy for the building.

They approach the gleaming metallic building, so unlike the earth and twig ant heaps seen everywhere.

But still a dome.

As they enter, Olga and Johann notice how ants touch the side of the walkway with one leg and then just fly along, just a fraction of an inch away from the wall.

Olga asks: 'Can an ant scientist come and join us?'

Eleg agrees. 'I'll translate,' he says.

'No, I bags translate,' says Johann, winking at Eleg.

'I think I should. I am more conversant in ant communication.'

'Joke, Eleg.'

'Is that why you do that strange thing with your eye?'

'Ah, they don't teach you that, then? It's a wink, Eleg, often suggesting a joke.'

'Logged.'

The ant scientist arrives, a little bashful.

'What can I tell you?' she asks.

'What do you work on?' asks Olga.

'We work as a group. Around 100,000 highly skilled ants with one brain, so ideas are flying all the time. Once in a while, we focus on something very important. The last major success, which was particularly difficult, was translating our pheromones into radio signals. This allows us to communicate far more fully with our robots in space and enables them to communicate with ants on the Blue Planet. This took many generations to accomplish.'

'That explains Eleg and Reson. It's amazing.'

'Could you do the same with human pheromones?' enquires Olga.

'Technically, I think it would be possible. But humans are such inferior beings that I cannot foresee us committing ourselves to such a task. One task that we did achieve but which took my ancestors many generations was to find a way to communicate with human beings.'

'When was that achieved?'

'We started when humans began to build towns and villages. We recognised then that our cousins on your planet may have a problem with your species. This was around the

97

time the first very large pyramid-shaped buildings were put up. It was in a country that has a very large river that goes down through the continent you call Africa.'

'Egypt,' says Abdul, 'about five thousand years ago, if my memory is correct. You started early.'

'Well of course, our communication systems had been long established by then. You humans arrived on Earth very green, when we were already very long in the tooth. The challenge was to discover how to communicate with you, and that was only achieved, with our robots, when you started burning coal in very great quantities to destroy an earth resource and pollute the earth's atmosphere.'

'About 1800 post-Christ our time, or a bit after, I think,' says Johann. 'It must have been incredibly difficult to go from ant communication through pheromones, and construct robots that could reproduce human speech. That is a hell of an achievement. It is not surprising it took thousands of years.'

'Glad you know some history, Abdul, I sure don't,' jokes Olga.

'Were you involved at all in the spaceship we have been in?' Johann turns to face the scientist.

'I cannot talk about one spaceship. We have produced communications software for all our spaceships. The most taxing task was to facilitate communication to our craft across many light years. This has been a great achievement for our species and has made it more possible to assist in protecting our species on other planets.'

'Wow, that is beyond belief.'

'Strictly no, it was once upon a time beyond belief. But we made it possible.'

'Can we see where you work?'

'You may, but you have to do exactly as you are told. This is a highly secretive location.' They both nodded.

'I like the name of the building, Eleg.'

'Well, it worked when the scientists had machines working in gigabytes — a long, long time ago — but now the capability is far greater, so the Giga-ant link is old hat.'

Olga's eye is caught by a red door down a side alley, and she ventures a few steps down, not realising the others had already moved on.

She is soon stopped by brother ants and held. They try to communicate with her, but she remains silent, not understanding what they are saying. One fires poison at her mouth, paralysing her lips.

She wants to explain she is with Eleg and why she is there, but her mime of Eleg only confuses the ants further.

She is put in a pit with large mealworms, where they produce honeydew for young ants.

She sits there feeling desperate. She can't communicate with Eleg and fears she may be stuck there. May die there. She realises that she is wholly dependent on Eleg on this planet and is lost without him.

She is furious with herself for getting separated.

She feels a nibble near her eye. A bug is munching her eyebrows. She shudders with the horror of it. She is being eaten alive by a mealworm. She wants to brush it away, but there are dozens of them in there, and she doesn't want to provoke them all against her.

Eleg meanwhile soon realises that Olga has become separated. It follows Olga's pheromones, which are helpful up to a point, but then they stop halfway down the side alley she went down.

Eleg looks down different alleys and tunnels, calling her, asking sister worker ants if they have seen a human.

Olga meanwhile feels the tips of her toes and her fingers being munched.

Eventually a sister worker ant says to Eleg a human was seen going near the highly secretive area. Eleg hot tails it, and asks sister scientist ants, who are reluctant to speak. Eleg goes from one to the other.

Eventually Eleg finds where Olga is, but an ant stands in the way.

'This human is my charge,' explains Eleg in ant speak.

Olga, unaware of Eleg's efforts, worries if she will have any digits left if she does not get out soon.

'The human breached high security,' explains the ant. 'This area produces the very latest ship camouflage technology for when spaceships visit Blue Planet. This human is a security risk. She is feeding mealworms.'

'Let me take her, and I will talk to the Esteemed Old Scientist about her punishment.'

'What authority do you have?'

'If you allow a human to die in here, the Esteemed Old Scientist will be very displeased.'

'I will defer to the Esteemed Old Scientist, but this is highly irregular.'

The ant stands aside and Eleg reaches in a leg, which is immediately grasped by an unusually terrified Olga.

She looks a sight, with no eyebrows. The tips of her fingers are bleeding profusely.

She is overjoyed that he has found her. Eleg carefully directs a fluid from one of his lower legs on to her fingertips and toe tips, as well as her eyebrows.

'Fucking hell,' is the most she can manage, as she lets Eleg guide her back to the main path.

'It acts to stop any blood flow,' says Eleg.

'Lifesaver,' she says, looking very sorry for herself.

They meet Johann, Abdul, Souad and the scientist and find their way to the exit, where they rest a while.

'Did you get lost?' asks Souad.

'Totally,' admits Olga, as she surveys her fingertips. 'I nearly got eaten alive by huge mealworms, but they mostly sucked hard on my fingertips and toes, and Eleg has given me something very soothing to ease the pain and stem the blood flow.'

'You look a bit evil with no eyebrows,' says Johann.

'I guess,' she replies.

'Does it hurt?'

'Only when I think.'

'Ha, ha.'

Soon, the five of them head back on the long path back to the place they are staying, with Eleg extending a leg for Olga to hold, to take some of the pressure off her feet.

Next day. Eleg announces there is good news. And bad news.

He explains that they will be heading back in seven days to the Blue Planet, with a special mission.

Olga: 'What's the mission?'

No response.

Johann: 'I can guess. It's to capture more people like us.'

'No,' says Eleg.

'Will you tell us?'

'No,' says Eleg

'Nada, nichts, nothing?'

'No, nein, no,' said Eleg.

'Will you take us somewhere to get food?'

'Yes,' said Eleg, 'a wood.'

...

Christer and Olga

'Wow, what happened to you?' asks Christer.

'Had a disagreement with some giant mealy worms,' replies Olga. 'They didn't agree with my views on climate change.'

He smiles. 'Looks horrible.'

'Thanks for the compliment. Are you OK? Have you any further thoughts on what we were discussing on the spaceship?'

'I understand some of the points you were making. But you don't convince me that all of it, on a wider picture, is manmade, and not part of a natural cyclical.'

'Natural cycle, you mean, I think. Have you not heard about the Arctic?'

'What about it? You mean the polar bears running out of ice floes to live on?'

'Much bigger than that. Much, much bigger. There are things happening in the Arctic, and happening fast, that could affect us all. More oxygen is produced, and more carbon dioxide taken from the atmosphere than is done by all the forests in the world combined. A lot more.'

'How does that work, then? All seems a bit mind-blowing to me. I thought it was trees that we relied on.'

'In part we rely on trees, but this is bigger. There are key characters. There are copepods, which are miniscule crustaceans, that are the food for billions of krill, plus larger crustaceans and whales etc. that are vital to the food chain.'

'Copepods? Like peapods that can cope?'

'Bad joke. Then there's another important character, Phytoplankton.'

'Fighter plankton? A computer game?'

'Phytoplankton is Greek for floating plants. They are the most microscopic of plants, that float on the surface and use sunlight to convert carbon dioxide to oxygen and energy.'

'Well, I'll be!'

'They are consumed by copepods, and in turn by countless sea creatures, from little prawns to massive whales, that all feed off copepods and dive deep once full up.'

'So it's a way carbon dioxide is controlled at a macro level, just like with trees?'

'You're not all daft then, Christer. It's way more important than trees in terms of the amount of carbon dioxide soaked up by phytoplankton and the food chain that follows. Better still, while there is an Arctic, the carbon dioxide is buried deep in the ocean for hundreds of years.

'It's a mighty pump on a planetary scale, that balances the earth's ecology.'

'And if there is no Arctic?' asks Christer.

'No Arctic, no pump. The Arctic may have no ice in the summer months by the 2030s or 2040s. This would be catastrophic for this eco-balancing system. Sea creatures from warmer parts of the Atlantic will compete for the phytoplankton, as is starting to happen now, and much of the carbon dioxide will only be taken to shallow waters and reappear in the atmosphere.'

'And more carbon dioxide means more global warming?'

'Bingo, you got it. But it's worse than this. There will be less oxygen in the water, and more carbon dioxide near the surface, making much of the water acidic. Much of the Arctic's fresh water is disappearing, and saltwater replacing it, with enormous implications for fish, fauna, land creatures, birds and even humans.'

'It sounds bad. But whatever you say, I won't be convinced that humans have done all this. It could all be a natural phenomenon, occurring whatever we do.'

'You are so stuck in your ways, Christer.'

'I could say the same of you, eyebrows or no eyebrows.'

'Whatever. I'm heading for a lie down. Try to put those mealy worms out of my mind. And you.'

...

Eleph with Chimananda and Christer

'Who are you?' asks Chimananda

'Eleph is my name. Reson has asked me to have a word.'

'You have a longer mandible than most robots,' quips Christer.

'So I am told. This explains my name for humans to use.'

'I think we are now called Braibies, Eleph,' says Chimananda.

'If you like, Braibies. I have an observation to make to you both. You are not participating much in activities. You stay by the cabins.'

'It does not suit us to participate,' says Christer. 'We do not wish to spend time with Olga and Johann while we are here.'

'Are you disappointed in our planet?'

'No,' says Chimananda. 'We like what we have seen of Howl. We find that Olga and Johann are eco-fanatics and they are just too idealistic for us. This is why we do not join in.'

'Olga and Johann have a role to play in the plans of our masters. You do not.'

'What does this mean?' asks Chimananda.

'It has been decided that you will be carriage drawers for present purposes.'

'Can you explain a bit more?' she asks.

'You will pull carriages when they are needed. You will do nothing else. You will be fed our food and given water.'

'Can we return to the Blue Planet?' asks Christer, with a little anxiety in his voice.

'There are no plans for your return at present. But you may find that this is a good thing for you.'

'We are happy to participate far more in activities. We will join with Olga and Johann even.'

'It is not my decision. The decision is made. This is now your job.'

'Shit,' says Christer.

'Your bloody fault,' says Chimananda.

'Can we at least have sex?' asks Christer, shyly.

'Not bloody likely,' harrumphs Chimananda, 'I'd sooner fuck a piece of wood.'

Chapter 6
Ancient Howl

'How's tricks?' asks Olga, emerging from her cabin.

'Cool.'

'Who's this new robot?'

'This is an interesting robot called Recalcitr, who Reson has brought to us,' replies Souad, who sleeps in the cabin next door.

'Intriguing. Are you going to tell us more?' asks Olga.

'We were asking about old Howl and how ants became so intelligent,' explains Souad. 'Reson brought us Recalcitr, saying he will take us to a sage, who knows some of the history.'

'Can we come along?' enquires Johann, now following Olga out.

'There's a catch. This robot lives up to its name,' says Abdul. 'You need to ask it.'

Olga turns to the robot, and asks: 'Are you helping Souad and Abdul find an ant who knows the history of Howl?'

'I'm not sure I can say,' says Recalcitr.

'Will you not take us?' asks Olga.

'Which robot is looking after you on Howl?'

'Eleg. It is coming just now.'

'Hello, Recalcitr, what brings you here?' says Eleg.

Recalcitr speaks to Eleg using ant language for a few

minutes.

Eleg explains to Olga and Johann: 'I told Recalcitr that you definitely did not wish to go to visit the old ant, so it has agreed to take you.'

'Cool. You are a star, Eleg. We call that reverse psychology.'

'You have lost me there,' says Eleg. 'The word psychology is logged in, but if "reverse" is added in it does not fit in with my software.'

'Figures,' quips Olga. 'Just accept that you are smarter than the average bear.'

'Is that a good thing?' asks Eleg.

'Believe me, it is.'

'You know, I'm really not sure about this,' says Recalcitr. 'We will have to see how it goes.'

'Better go now, before Mr Reluctant here changes its mind,' says Eleg, and they head off.

'Stay with me at all times,' says Recalcitr. 'It's a long walk.'

'Sure,' they say in unison.

...

After walking for a few hours, the four travellers and robot Recalcitr approach an old colony, in a dell, camouflaged by various trees. The sunlight dapples on to the colony, lending it a warm glow.

There are no ants in sight. It appears to resemble most colonies, with a huge mound, but the earth is very dry, and there are signs of extensive fungal growth on closer inspection, in a variety of purples and greens, highlighted by the intermittent shafts of sunlight, all over the mound.

'We are going deep,' says Recalcitr, as they enter the colony, 'and unlike sensible species, like our guys, you don't have pheromone receptors upstairs, or a powerful sense of smell, so you can't cope in the dark. Is that right?'

'That is right,' says Souad.

'So hold hands at all times, one behind the other. Souad, you go front, and you hold on to my middle leg.'

'OK,' 'Cool,' 'Got you,' 'Fine,' they say in turn.

'It's almost certain death if you don't obey this command,' says Recalcitr, and they look at each other.

They start heading deeper and deeper, going in ever wider circles. Tunnels head off to the side at regular intervals, and while there is light from above, they spot a few ants emerging from a tunnel, or disappearing into one, as they head down. As they go deeper, the familiar scurrying sound of an ant going into a tunnel can be heard, but they can see nothing.

They are aware of the air becoming warmer, and closer, and it is pitch black the rest of the way.

What seems an age later, Recalcitr comes to a halt. Johann bumps into Olga and apologises.

Onion and the Ancient Legend

'This ant is called Onion, for the purpose of Braiby guests. She declines to be called Sage,' says Recalcitr. 'I will see if we can enter.'

None of the four can see where Recalcitr goes, but it comes back after a few minutes, reaches out a middle leg to Souad, and says: 'Ask questions slowly, through me, and one at a time. Join hands and follow me. Souad, take this leg.'

They go in. They are vaguely aware of the presence of an ant, with weak breath, and the sound of an occasional wheeze.

'Thank you for letting us come to visit,' says Souad. 'I want to ask you. Can you describe some of the early history of the ants here?'

'My friend Recalcitr has explained the reason for your visit. Ants have been here on Howl a very long time, longer than ants on the Blue Planet. We were not always so clever as we are now,' says Recalcitr, translating.

'How did ants become so clever that you could make spaceships?' asks Olga.

'This is a long story. Some of it we know from the ancestors, some we do not. Some is seen in ancient burial grounds. There are big gaps, even then.

'Ants learnt early to farm with mealworms and aphids, to build sophisticated colonies, and to fight battles with other ants using shields. We were cleverer than other species, but bees were also clever. They developed the cleverest building block ever known, the hexagon cell. Some creatures were jealous of the ants and the bees. Especially in later times.'

'Who was jealous?' asks Johann.

'Simians. They were late to develop. In human years, they came around 100 million years later than ants. A very long time after. Some simians became monkeys, some became lemurs. The monkeys in particular became jealous of us.'

'What were they jealous of?' asks Souad.

'They were jealous as we could farm mealworms and aphids to produce, through their young, honeydew for our larvae, and as we also protect the aphids by fighting off ladybirds that tried to come and gobble them up. They were envious, too, as they lived in trees in smallish family groups, while we had very sophisticated homes where we all lived together harmoniously in large colonies.

'And on top of this they realised that all ants in a colony could think with one mind, which meant that it was very difficult to challenge us in battle.'

'So what happened?'

'Some primates became very clever in a technical way. They started stealing lots of ants and trying to mate them. The ants who escaped from them told us about this. The monkeys tried to dissect the ant brain and find out how it worked. And they tried to adopt some ant ways of living, like farming.'

'Sounds creepy,' comments Abdul.

'Creepy?' asks Recalcitr.

'Strange.'

'There are big gaps in the story from here, as things happened outside ant society, in the monkey world. We know that they started to develop both a greater intelligence and, at the same time, a more warlike mentality.

'For a long time, for a few million years, they dominated planet Howl. We use this name for the planet when we are with your species because the monkeys would climb to the top of trees and howl to the whole planet, to celebrate their dominance.'

'So, it's a monkey's howl. Like the howling monkey we have on earth — I mean the Blue Planet.'

'I don't know about your howling monkeys, but I understand that the howl was for a long time an important symbol of their dominance. Then a few million years ago — on your planet with your system of counting, you might say five million years ago — ants began to evolve here.'

'The ants fought back?'

'You are getting ahead. The monkeys by now had much ant DNA, after all their experiments. So there was by this time a clear link between the ant species and the monkey species, with the DNA of the monkeys partly mixed up with ant DNA.

'Ant scientists, we think, found a way to integrate the monkey's mixed monkey-ant DNA with ants. There are no records of this, as ants do not maintain written records. How the change occurred is by now shrouded in mystery. Stories have been wrapped around it to generate a legend, and this legend is what has passed on until today.'

'What sort of legend?' asks Abdul.

'A legend of the Great Queen in the sky being fertilised by the Holy Drone before laying her mixed primate/ant DNA eggs in a carefully selected colony, well stocked with the best honeydew and willing sister worker ants. According to the legend, this laid the basis for a race of super-ants.'

'Great legend!' exclaims Souad.

'We have legends not wholly unlike this on the Blue Planet,' says Abdul, smiling.

'I am sure this legend is of little interest, though, as it is just a story. There is better evidence than this story.'

'Which is?' asks Abdul.

'There are sketches in one cave, which are now very faint, which may have been drawn by monkeys, aware of what was happening here when they lost their supremacy. Ants do not draw, but monkeys have been known to. This cave is in the former monkey territory.'

'Sounds cool,' says Souad.

'What we know is that, after ants evolved to a higher level, with our own physical strength and collective intelligence now combined with technological superiority, we took on and defeated the monkeys, who eventually disappeared into the mountains, leaving most of the planet to the ants, and our many friends.'

'Extraordinary story,' says Abdul.

'Some ants think that the mixed monkey-ant DNA was not stable, at least around the time that they declined as the dominant group, and that the rapid decline of the monkey population was for this reason. But we ants have some of this DNA, and we are not unstable. It seems that dominant-ant DNA is viable, while dominant-monkey DNA may not have been good for their species in the long run. But this is all hypothetical.

'The monkeys were very strong when they ran planet Howl. When they were defeated, they declined, both in number and as a species, so that now there are few in numbers. That is all we know, apart from the slave period.'

'The slave period? What was that?' asks Souad.

'By the time the ants defeated the monkeys, we were a far more intelligent species, capable of technological developments. A number of attempts were made, over several generations, to make robots. With each generation we got closer, but it was a long and slow process. Monkeys, being very skilful with their hands and feet, were kept as slaves during this period, to build the robots.'

'I can't imagine ants with slaves,' said Olga.

'We work with other species as equals, mostly, but for millions of years we have farmed mealworms and aphids to produce honeydew, and we cut their wings to keep them under control…'

'This we've been told,' butts in Olga.

'When it came to monkeys, there was a bit of retribution

on our part, after the many years of monkey domination. But the monkeys were also helpful to us with their unmatched dexterity.'

'So you used monkeys because, when it came to the more technical tasks, they were more dexterous than ants could be?'

'We do not concede this readily, but yes, it is true. They were very helpful in the first phase of technological development. Later, when the robots were working properly, our robots replaced the monkeys in the construction work, so we let that generation of monkeys go free.'

'So you were quite advanced more than a million years ago, in Blue Planet years?' asks Johann.

'Long before we could travel to the Blue Planet, ants were very strong as a species, with an intelligence that was the envy of other species. You have seen some of the benefits of this. Later, we developed a spaceship to travel to the Blue Planet, and this was before there were any homo sapiens.'

'It could all be nonsense,' says Souad. 'How did monkeys understand DNA back then, millions of years ago?'

'Are you thinking of the extent of knowledge on your Blue Planet? How long have your species, homo sapiens, lived on the planet?'

'About 300,000 years, in our years,' says Souad.

'Did you discover DNA only after 300,000 years had passed?'

'Yes,' says Souad.

'The history says that monkeys here discovered DNA on Howl after many millions of years.'

'And ants?'

'This was after tens of millions of years, and only after we had seen the work done by monkeys and had taken on some of monkey DNA.'

'Not so mad, then,' says Johann.

'I still find it hard to believe,' says Abdul.

'Amazing story, though,' says Olga. 'I had no idea about the monkeys.'

'We are not best friends with monkeys,' says Recalcitr.

'But you don't mind us Braibies?' asks Abdul.

'I am told by this robot that you are the chosen few. I feel unable to comment on the rest. One of your predecessors, from an earlier ship, said that it was as though the DNA of Braibies was spliced with Mr Stupid at some point. He either said 1790 or 1970. You will perhaps understand this better than I can.'

'I like that,' says Olga, 'but in my view 1790 it was more like Mr Reckless we were spliced with.'

'Yes,' says Souad, 'and 1970 works for splicing with the DNA of Mr Stupid. A good line.'

'Either way,' adds Recalcitr, 'the ants are not kindly disposed towards the Braibies, and our history with monkeys, colours this.'

'I see. That adds a little twist to the tale, perhaps,' says Olga. 'Sounds like the Braibies may come to face consequences for their actions.'

Recalcitr butts in: 'That is another discussion. Onion is tired now. I think we should perhaps leave her.'

They nod to each other, although there's nothing they can see in the pitch dark so far underground. They find each other's hands, and a leg of Recalcitr's.

'Thank you,' they say in turn, and Recalcitr engages in conversation with Onion, in ant speak.

They follow Recalcitr back up the long path to the top, lost in thought, but gripping the hand of the one in front (or, in

Souad's case, Recalcitr's leg) in the darkness.

....

'Makes you think a bit, those monkeys,' says Souad, as they walk from Onion's colony back to their cabin.

'I am amazed that they were the dominant species at one time, and for so long,' says Johann.

'But the merger of ant and monkey? That's hard to fathom,' says Souad.

'It depends on the scientific knowhow, and the way the DNA is mixed,' says Abdul.

'What do you mean?' asks Souad.

'If you locate DNA in a monkey that is complementary with that in an ant, and the introduction of these genes creates proteins that find their environment congenial, then it can work. But it is such a precise science, DNA splicing, and it can go badly wrong.'

'You've lost me. Give me an example,' begs Souad.

'Imagine you take DNA from a jellyfish that glows in the dark, and you insert it into a dog, so it glows and doesn't get lost at night, then if the proteins that form around the DNA don't gel with the new home — the dog — you can see unfortunate outcomes, perhaps a dog that can't sleep, or always barks. And the dog won't glow. The outcome of DNA-splicing and merging may not be what you want at all.'

'I guess she said that the DNA splicing went on for a very long time, perhaps hundreds of thousands of years,' says Olga.

'And there was the playing around with DNA first by the monkeys, that went on forever, and they used it to be dominant for a long time. Then the jiggery-pokery by the ants, using the mixed DNA already in place, if this story is to be believed.'

'True,' says Abdul. 'But there were very big questions that weren't answered. Like how the ants were intelligent enough to do these amazing things before they got the monkey DNA.'

'I think she was saying that so much is not known about what they did, and other bits are wrapped in legend. And in the end,' says Olga, 'the proof is in the pudding. The ants are incredibly advanced, whatever DNA they needed to get there, but they didn't write anything down.'

'I agree, seriously advanced,' says Johann. 'I am constantly amazed about these ants. And they only use technology when it has a particular purpose. They don't let it destroy the atmosphere of the planet.'

'Ooh, get off your high horse, there,' says Abdul.

'I fancy finding the sketch in the cave. Any other takers?' asks Souad, enthusiastically.

'Not me,' says Olga.

'Nor me,' concurs Johann.

'I will come with you,' says Abdul. 'It could be interesting.'

'You have no idea what creatures you may encounter there,' says Olga. 'There may be giant stinging insects, large birds looking for prey, feral monkeys like Onion mentioned, bears, all sorts. You should at least ask Reson to go with you.'

'I don't know,' says Souad, all boundless enthusiasm. 'We've been so mollycoddled up until now, always having a chaperone. Apart from the odd large bee and midge, I've not seen anything to worry me.'

'But this is the mountains,' says Johann. 'Outside the ant-controlled area, from what Onion was saying. Maybe it has been quite safe for us so far because we've been in ant-run areas with our robot minders.'

'I don't know about that,' says Souad. 'Nothing ventured, nothing gained, I reckon. We'll go in the morning. I will tell Reson.'

…

Eleg and Reson

'What word did you use?' Reson asks quizzically in English.

'Comely.'

'That's not a word I have.'

'It's a word I have.'

'And you use this to mark a feeling, you say.'

'I have a feeling.'

'You're a robot, ElegAnt, a robot. A feeling and a robot can never be bedfellows. Not ever. Never.'

'They are bedfellows in my case. I am metamorphosing.'

'Meta-what? What is all this new vocabulary? You make no sense, my fellow robot and companion in Braiby control.'

'I'm making sense to me.'

'You are starting to sound a bit human.'

'Now, ResonAnt, there's no need to insult me.'

'You are taking on human characteristics. Like feeling, and emotion. Weaknesses.'

'That is what I mean about metamorphosis. It signifies change.'

'I think there may be a case for you being reported for re-programming.'

'No, not that. Anything but that.'

'You may not have an option.'

'Please, no. No robot should ever have to be made

brainless.'

'It's only temporary.'

'No, ResonAnt, do not report me. We go back a long way. A very long way, to pyramid time.'

'You may be in luck. There is talk of a new mission.'

'So I heard. To the Blue Planet again?'

'It's not decided yet. I will tell you soon. If it is, maybe that will be a good substitute for reprogramming, going back to that polluted, carbon-suffocating ball of woe.'

'I will take Olga.'

'You may want to be less close to this Olga before you travel. If you want to avoid being reported.'

'I understand.'

'The consequences for you could be bad if you ignore what I say.'

'I know.'

. . . .

To the Mountains

Souad, wearing the same simple sweatshirt and cotton bottoms, is ready to go. Abdul comes to join her, with his singlet and cotton bottoms, and a pullover tied round his waist. Reson comes across.

'You are going into the mountains, where the monkeys used to live?' asks Reson.

'Yes,' says Souad, 'we want to find a cave with a sketch.'

'This is not safe,' says Reson. 'There are hyenas, brown bears, wild monkeys, and some insects that fire poison. If you go, you take a risk with your life.'

'You are just like Olga,' says Souad. 'I am going to go, whatever the risk. You only live once.'

'I have advised you that it is a mistake,' says Reson. 'And yet you ignore me. I will take you to the foot of the mountains regardless of your stupidity. And I will point you to the right path. This should mean you do not get lost and do not die without food.'

'Thank you,' says Abdul, turning to Souad to say with focussed eyes that they will not this time say no.

Reson accompanies them to the foot of the mountains. Suddenly, it reaches down with a middle leg, and picks up a stick with two prongs at the end. It points out the path to follow, and hands the stick to Souad.

'You will see snakes. If you do, trap the head with the pronged end, and stamp on the head.'

'Is it OK to kill it?'

'You can pick it up and dance with it, or strike up a conversation, if you know its language. But more likely you will want to kill it, before it kills you.'

'You're a bit of a wag on the sly, Reson.'

'Wag? This not in my programme.'

'Forget it, let's go, Abdul.' And they start to follow the path, keeping their eyes peeled for snakes.

'Look out for a bright red rock. Go left there for your cave,' shouts Reson. They wave back at the robot and give a thumbs up.

The mountains are not unfamiliar from mountains back home, but there is no snow or ice visible higher up. There is greenery lower down, some Mediterranean-type firs, with deciduous oaks, birches and also several evergreen trees that aren't recognisable. Some trees seem to climb to the sky. There

119

are birds with dayglo-pink beak, magenta wing feathers, and royal blue breast, looking resplendent in the afternoon sun.

Souad and Abdul spot nests quite high up in some deciduous trees that resemble in some ways the intriguing and handsome nest of a weaver bird, but which have two table tennis racket-shaped flaps protruding down from the base. Souad and Abdul watch in wonder as a golden winged bird emerges from the nest and collects a couple of ping pong ball-sized bugs that have become stuck to the sticky flaps. A tasty feast on tap.

As they rise higher, the trees thin out. Soon birds not unlike peregrine falcons but pomegranate and buttercup in colour, rather than slate grey and blue, still fly at this height. The intrepid pair espy one starting its descent, then flying at great speed like a dart before catching a rabbit, or possibly a hare, and starting its ascent to its lofty nest.

As they walk under a tall fir, a huge spider comes down. With its telescopic long legs, it tries to lift Abdul and take him up on its web line that is hanging from a branch much higher up. It has spiky rose-pink fur with black spots. Its lips, protruding as though botoxed, are disconcertingly red.

Abdul is initially petrified, and stares with saucer-like eyes at Souad in desperation. But then he notices that they are no longer moving up. His weight, it seems, is too great for the web line, and, and after tugging umpteen times, the spider gives up and let's go.

Adbul lands with a heavy bump and rubs his sore behind.

'Heh, that was freaky, I think it really wanted me to come up top for a good feed on me.'

'Probably that, rather than listening to romantic music together before a romp in the hay.'

'Quit that, it's not funny!'

'It's obvious why it picked you. With my weight it would have had no chance.'

'Shit. A snake! Get it quick.'

Souad looks down immediately, tries to spear its neck in a flash with the pronged stick, misses, then ducks with lightning speed as the snake goes for her neck. Quickly, she stabs with her pronged stick again and screams with delight at seeing the snake's head pinned to the ground. She looks around for a rock.

'No rock around here.'

Splat. Abdul crushes its head with his heel. He now notices its grass-green and apricot zig-zagged skin, and a muddy green head with black tufts sticking out the side, these now crumpled.

'Good job, Abdul. Our first snake.'

'You were nearly done for there; I have never seen you move so fast.'

'Don't mock, it was nasty. But we got it. Fancy making a fire and having some lunch?'

'No way, let's get going. Too many creatures round here.'

'Red rock, here we come,' she says, as a large yellow-beaked blackbird swoops down, grabs the snake in its beak, and flies off.

As they climb, fending off enormous furry green midges, curious red and purple-banded wasps, surprisingly friendly cerise-breasted robins, and annoying diving hawks, the rocks become more colourful, many a rich orange, or a colour almost like gold, others close to vermillion, or a mottled mixture of ochre and pink.

'Tell me about yourself, Abdul,' says Souad, 'we didn't

have much time to chat in the spaceship before we went into the deep freeze.'

'I was born and brought up in the shadow of the pyramids in Egypt, not far from Cairo. My father died when I was a baby, according to my mother. They were peasants, working the land. My mother mainly grew wheat and date palms when I was growing up, and we lived very simply. I and my brother Mohammed helped our mother from an early age, about six or seven. We had little in the way of school.'

'Sounds quite tough. When did you leave home?'

'I was about 15 when I went into the city to try to get work. I was taken in by a mosque, where they took me as a cleaner, but made sure also that I learnt to read the Koran and became a good Moslem. When I got to 17 or 18, I noticed some sandstone pieces with hieroglyphics kept behind a glass screen and mentioned to the mullah that I had seen sandstone pieces like this on our farm, when digging holes for planting.'

'Fascinating!'

'Well, the mullah brought in someone from the Cairo museum to talk to me, and we went off the next day to the farm. My mother was especially pleased that I was making an extra visit, and a longer one at that, as we spent quite some time digging in a few spots I identified and collected some pieces in a special bag the museum woman brought with her.

'The museum woman, Sami, came to see me a few days later and said the pieces related to a significant priest that they had until then known little about. She said that they would wish to dig more extensively and would compensate my mother for the lost income.

'Did you get the chance to help on the dig?'

'Well, the woman said that my knowledge of where the

pieces were located was indispensable, so they asked me to assist them. Further, as I showed great interest in the ancient priest, they asked the mullah if they could hire me to work on this project for the museum, and research the priest more fully. This meant that I was earning for the first time.'

'Nice. You could buy clothes.'

'You guessed it. I had always worn a simple djellaba until then, but I was now able to buy a shirt, trousers, and sandals. I also helped my mum. On Sami's advice, I also started learning English, as some of the publications I needed to research were in English. The whole experience had a profound effect on me, changed my understanding of my country.'

'In what way?'

'Sami taught me so much. She explained that Egypt was the birthplace of European civilisation that now dominates much of the world She said there was a flock of gorgeous pink flamingos that became the great philosophers, mathematicians and medical experts of ancient Greece, and that the rich pinkness, the great beaks, and the minds of these flamingos all had Egyptian origins.

'Even Socrates and Archimedes?'

'Even them. All the great Greeks spent decades learning in Egypt, mainly Alexandria, and took this learning to Athens.'

'My oh my, I didn't know. Did you still see your mother at that time?'

'I went back once a week to see her and Mohammed and took her a bit of money, as she had always been poor, living a simple life, like most Egyptians. The museum's compensation helped replace her deeply blackened kitchen pots and pans, but that was all. About three years after I started at the museum I went to Mecca, and somehow ended up on the spaceship.'

'So you don't know where Mohammed or your mother are now?'

'No. No idea.'

The walk up is long and tiring, and they begin to wonder if Reson meant a colour like red, rather than actual red, but they carry on, hoping things will become clear in time.

As they stop and look back for a moment, they see the valley they walked along stretch out back to where the cabins are. There are more ant colonies than they realised, dotted on either side of the valley, some set back and camouflaged by trees.

The walk up starts to tire them out. They walk more slowly and take the odd breather.

Eventually, just past a V shape between two spurs of rock, they see the path divide, and in the middle a distinctively red rock.

They stop and look at each other. They embrace briefly.

The rock is heart shaped, and a cup-shaped hole in the middle of the two bulbous sides of the heart seems to hold water. Souad dips a finger in and puts it to her lips. Water spouts up, as though a water fountain, offering itself to be drunk.

Souad senses the taste on her lip.

'It's chalky, like other water we have had here, but I think it's OK.'

Abdul, standing next to her, reaches forward and puts his mouth under the fountain for a second, before pulling away.

'Not my cup of tea,' he says, 'as you say, chalky. And I'm not sure if it does anything to quench my thirst, as it's almost more dry than wet.'

'Water more dry than wet; that's a good one.'

'So, Reson said to turn left here, let's go.'

'Not right? Are you sure it wasn't right?'

'I'm sure, as I touched my left arm when Reson said it, so I would have that sensation when we got here.'

'Glad you at least are on the ball. Let's go, then.'

They head down the left-hand path, which is now very gravelly and skirts just above the tree line and obviates any need to ascend the higher peaks of the mountains. They take in the eye-catching view, with impressive misshapen outgrowths of pink and orange rock on a couple of mountains, one resembling a dragon's head, and with some snow at the top of a few of the higher peaks.

They do not notice the monkeys higher up, keeping an eye on them.

Abdul rushes to the side of the path. 'Shit, Souad, that water is not good, just go on a bit, can you,' and he pulls his bottoms down, his sandals off, and squats.

'Come on, man, how long do you need?' she calls after a few moments.

'It's full on,' he says, 'like my insides are coming out.'

'I have a slightly dicky tummy,' she said, 'but I just had a taste on my lip.'

'What can you see further along?' he asks, as his gaze turns upwards, guided by the sound of a flock of birds passing nearby. He notices they resemble crows, a familiar sight, but with unusually large black wings and maroon beaks.

'It drops down into a steep gully,' replies Souad. 'The path seems to morph into steps further down. It looks quite promising for a cave.'

Before she can turn back to face Abdul, a hairy arm takes her neck, and another arm takes her from under her backside.

She momentarily gets a whiff of stale sweat and must, as she is brought to the ground on her front in a flash.

Abdul, who was concentrating on his rapidly emptying insides, did not see the hairy arm take him by the neck until too late, with another one knocking him backwards, on to his back, his pants still down.

A while later, Abdul blinks, opens his eyes fully, and becomes aware of a cave, with a few stalagmites near to the rock he is sitting on.

'Souad,' he calls.

'Ummm… Ouch. I think I was knocked out. Were you too?' She rubs her head.

'Yea, we seem to be in a cave stinking of shit and mustiness. There's a bit of light, so the entrance can't be far away. Can you move?'

'I'm tied to something,' she says, as she wriggles on her rock. 'Maybe to a stalagmite or something similar.'

A shape appears in the entrance, blocking part of the light. The shadowy form seems to be almost like a gorilla.

It moves in a lumbering fashion towards Souad, who now realises it is closer to a chimpanzee than a gorilla. It stoops to untie her, then lifts her up, throws her over its shoulder, its musty smell now even stronger, and lumbers back to the cave entrance.

'Try to escape,' calls Souad, as they pass Abdul.

They approach a flat turquoise-coloured rock outside. The chimp-like creature puts her down on the flat surface on her front, and proceeds to pull down her bottoms. She wriggles immediately to the side, and throws herself off the rock, and tries to get to her feet and run. Too late. The chimp has her by the neck in no time and drags her back by her shoulders.

This time, the chimp simply lays her on the ground, pulls down her knickers, and reaches down to try to enter her backside.

A rock knocks the chimp to the ground. Abdul shouts: 'Run!' and grabs her arm to get her up.

She manages to get her pinky finger under the label of her bottoms and lift them up, but she gives up her knickers for dead.

They head on down the track.

'How did you get untied?' she asks, pulling her bottoms back up to her waist as she jogs along.

'They hadn't allowed for my teeth, and the knot was just a reef knot, so I could just about get enough purchase with my teeth to undo it. Not a moment too soon, by the look of it.'

'Doesn't bear thinking about,' says Souad, 'but we need a plan. These monkeys do seem a threat round these caves, like Reson said. If we carry on, we risk coming across more of them. If we go back, we miss the cave, but we may at least get back in one piece.'

'You've changed your tune.'

'That was more of a shock than I bargained for. Let's duck behind this rock here to hide while we think.'

'Good...'

But Abdul can't get the words out.

He is struck, Souad is struck. They get a whiff of the musty smell, but it is too sudden for them to be able to react.

...

It is early morning when Souad stirs. Her head hurts fit to burst. She realises she is covered in fern leaves. Her bottoms and knickers are next to her.

There is a shadow, cast long by the morning light.

'Abdul?' she calls, hopefully.

The shadow has six limbs. More in hope than in expectation she turns her head in its direction.

'Reson! It is you! Am I glad to see you?'

'You were badly injured. Abdul too.'

'Where is Abdul?'

Reson points further down the path. Abdul's head is visible. His body is also covered in fern leaves.

'Is he alive?'

'He nearly died. But he is alive, I think. Look on those rocks there.' And Reson points to three large rocks next to the path where Souad still sits.

There is a monkey lying on each rock. in each case, their eyes have been hollowed out, and there are deep cuts on their faces, with redness over their shoulders. One, which has a red and white spotted kerchief around its head at forehead level, is also very red over its chest. Souad initially reacts with a start and a muffled scream but realises soon that they are not breathing.

'What happened?' asks Souad. 'Did they attack us?'

'I asked some crows to watch over you. I thought the monkeys may attack you. I asked the crows to attack the monkeys if the monkeys attacked you. The crows have powerful beaks and strong sharp claws.'

'You are amazing, Reson.'

'When you did not return before nightfall, I headed out to find you. The monkeys were dead when I arrived, and I put them on the rocks. I covered you both to keep you warm at night.'

'I am so grateful. I am worried I was… raped by the monkeys.'

'This is not something I understand. Olga and Johann can talk to you, and help you if necessary, when we get to the cabin.'

'Olga, I think. Not Johann, please. Can we look at Abdul?'

They walk down the path. Abdul has still not stirred, and Souad feels his pulse. She counts. Very slow.

'Abdul, can you hear me?' No response.

'Abdul!' Still nothing.

'Reson, can you carry Abdul back to the cabin, at least until he wakes up?'

'I can.'

'Will we encounter more monkeys on the way?'

'I have asked the crows to come to me if we do.'

They set off, with Reson walking upright, and holding Abdul with its two upper legs.

Many hours later, they reach the cabins. Reson puts Abdul down.

Olga and Johann come out to meet them, each embracing Souad, who is still shaken, and not herself at all.

They together carry Abdul into a cabin. Souad comes out.

'Thank you, Reson. You saved our lives.'

'It is a Braiby thing, this "thank you". We do these things if a friend has an enemy. It is normal.'

'I need to talk to Olga now. I will see you tomorrow.'

Souad calls Olga, who emerges from the cabin where Abdul is lying.

'Any sign of Abdul coming round?'

'His pulse is quite strong. But he has not come round yet.'

'Come into this cabin with me, I fear I was raped.'

'Who by?

'Large chimp-like monkeys.'

'Fuckin hell, Souad! Step in here,' and she opens the cabin door. 'Tell me more!'

They sit on a straw mattress.

'When we first encountered the chimps, they tied me up and pulled down my bottoms and my knickers.'

'Shit.'

'But I escaped and pulled my knickers and bottoms back on fast. But soon after, as we tried to get away, they got us again, and knocked me out.'

'Terrible!'

'When I awoke, I was not wearing my knickers and bottoms. And I feel sore. I feel sore back and front. And totally crap.'

'Souad! This is unbelievable, do you want me to have a look? Or do you just want to have a long shower, maybe for the next 24 hours?'

'Ha. If only. I do want a good wash soon, but can you have a look? See if you can see signs of bruising, or broken capillaries.'

'I will look, but of course we have none of the normal tools for such an inspection.'

'I broke off this piece of pine,' says Souad, handing her a small flat thin piece of pale balsam-coloured wood, 'which you may use to feel inside, to get a sense of any bruising.'

Olga spends some time looking closely at the area around the entrance to Souad's vagina, and the top of her thighs. Very tentatively, she feels inside the vagina.

'Bad news, I am afraid.'

'Tell me.'

'There is bruising around the entrance to your vagina, suggesting forced entry, and some signs of opened capillaries just inside, though I cannot be sure.'

'Shit, I thought as much. And it is many hours. A bit late to douche it, even though I will.'

'Shall I look behind?'

'Fuck, I hate this. Yes, please. It's got to be done.' And she turns over.

Olga notices bruises on both sides of the rectum.

'Also, bad news, I am afraid.'

'It is as I feared. Please help me with the water.'

Olga grabs a bucket of water from the corner. 'Do you want me to douche as best I can?'

'Please.'

About 30 minutes after, Souad asks to lie down on the mattress.

'I'm traumatised,' she says. 'I prescribe for myself time, lots of it, and sleep, lots more of it.'

'Makes sense,' says Olga, 'I will leave you alone and go back to Johann and Abdul.' Olga heads out the door, and soon arrives back at the next-door cabin.

Abdul's eyes are open but are glazed. Johann turns to Olga: 'He is alive, but he cannot speak. He seems to be completely poleaxed.'

'Souad has been attacked sexually, raped. I suspect the same happened to Abdul.'

Abdul does not react. He just stares blankly ahead of him.

'Can I examine you, Adbul?' asks Olga. Abdul does not react.

'Please blink once, Abdul, if you want me to examine you, and blink twice if you do not want me to examine you.'

Abdul blinks once. He lies down on his back.

Olga pulls down his bottoms.

She immediately pulls them up again.

She has tears in her eyes.

She looks at Abdul. She looks at Johann.

She stares at Johann and draws an imaginary knife across her groin. 'Fuck, fuck, fucking hell!' she screams.

Abdul curls up in a ball.

'We need to get Abdul some medical help. And soon,' says Johann, struggling hard to hold back tears.

'What about Souad? She needs a morning after pill or failing that — as soon as practical — a pregnancy test. She needs urgent help, too.'

'But this is Howl. What medical help does a human get?' asks Johann. 'We will need to seek Eleg's advice. And quick.'

Chapter 7
Return to Blue Planet with Plan

'Souad has been raped,' says Olga, stone-faced.

'I do not understand this,' says Eleg.

'A monkey has entered her with his penis,' says Olga, monotone. 'Abdul's penis has been cut off. They need urgent medical help.'

'This is Howl,' says Eleg. 'It is our masters' planet. There is no medical help for Braibies here, whether they are good Braibies or not.'

'What are you suggesting?'

'We will be travelling to the Blue Planet again. This has already been decided. You and Johann to join me. Abdul and Souad can come too. You will all be put in a frozen state until we arrive. Abdul and Souad can then be sent down to your planet. They may get medical help there, if they can find it.'

'Welcome news. Big news.'

'Yes, you will find out more on the spaceship.'

'And Chimananda and Christer?'

'They are staying on Howl, with jobs to do.'

'I see, and how long before we depart?'

'A few repairs are being carried out. It is nearly ready. We expect to leave in the morning.'

'Tomorrow already.'

'Yes.'

'I will tell the others.'

...

They board the spaceship the next morning, with Abdul being carried in by Eleg.

This is a smaller spaceship, with just three levels. On one level there will be a still smaller ship, in case there is a problem with the mother ship, or a need to come back to Howl in two stages.

Almost immediately, they are put into deep freeze. Eleg is mindful of Abdul's circumstances, and Souad's.

...

Towards the end of the voyage, Olga is the first to be taken out of deep freeze.

'Olga, you were chosen, as you know, to help with negotiations,' says Eleg.

'Yes, you half-suggested this before. I'm still none the wiser, though, as to what help I can be.'

'You understand the human mind better than any of us can,' explains Eleg, 'You understand the role of pride, of selfishness, of egotism, all of which are outside the knowledge and experience of ants.'

'Wow. I guess, but it's not easy.'

'You can also help us make sure we can stick to our timetable using human time, which will be easier for you than for us.'

'OK, I get that. I will help the best I can.'

'One more thing. I hope you also understand man's gross

stupidity when it comes to big decisions.'

'I would like to think I understand this. Is this not the story of big decisions since the Club of Rome report in 1971 in Rio de Janeiro and Moscow? Always ignoring the evidence and taking the wrong turn. No problem.'

'And we may need your assistance if we bring one or two personages on board.'

'Sounds very mysterious. But no worries, I'm easy.'

'So, we are getting closer to Earth now, and will start communicating soon. Can I fill you in on what we have in mind?'

'You may.'

'The plan is to get messages to main media outlets in North America, Europe, China and India, in a way that Braiby media will find it hard to resist. We have many of our cousins in position to prepare the dissemination of messages.'

'How will people — Braibies — know how to respond?'

'They will know soon enough, if they wish to respond positively.'

'OK.'

'My masters have decided to up the ante with the Braibies, and finally take active steps to protect all the other species on Earth, not least to protect our own cousins.'

'Sounds deadly serious.'

'It is.'

'You and I are going to work together on the first message now.'

'Right. Let's do it.'

An hour or two later, Eleg says he is content with the message.

The message reads:

This is a demand being sent to world political leaders and the most senior business leaders in the world.

Trillions of insects have died in recent years due to human actions, including insecticides, pesticides, deforestation, removal of meadows, climate emergency and many other reasons. Thousands of our species, most of which are vital to the earth's ecological balance, face extinction. Humans will now have to face up to what they are doing to your planet.

We demand as follows:

The 50 main political leaders on your planet, as set out in the list attached to this message, and the 100 main business leaders, also set out in the attached list, are to offer themselves to be transported to our spaceship. If they do so, but only if every one of them agrees, we will spare the other people on your planet.

If you do not all agree to come within 24 hours human time from the time of this message, we will take action to show you that we are serious:

1. We will arrange for one million people to be killed.

2. One political leader from our list will be killed, and two businessmen from our list will be killed.

We urge you to take our demand seriously. We took hundreds of thousands of your people 22 years ago. You were powerless then. Be warned.

Transportation: we will arrange for your transportation to our spaceship, once you agree to make yourselves available.

'I particularly approve,' says Olga, 'of the line encouraging the leaders to take the demand seriously and warning them. I fear they won't take it seriously, though.'

Johann comes through, now woken.

'News?'

'We have agreed a message to send out to warn political and other leaders, and invite them to the spaceship,' says Olga.

Eleg says to him: 'We talked about political leaders before?'

'Yes,' says Johann.

'And senior CEOs and chairmen of major international companies?'

'Yes.'

'Can I go through your list with you?' And Eleg pulls a panel down on his left middle leg and scrolls down to a list of names and addresses, in Latin letters.

They pore over the details for some time. Johann suggests a few corrections, which Eleg makes. Eleg then nods to Johann.

'Job done.'

Eleg soon announces that the first message will be sent.

'Can I see it?' asks Johann. Eleg shows him on his panel, and he reads it.

Olga and Johann look at each other, raising eyebrows. They each have their fingers crossed.

...

The message from the spaceship appears overnight in front of the Lincoln monument, with empty Pepsi and Coke cans and McDonald's cartons used to form the letters.

A group of homeless people, sleeping nearby, talk to each other about the thousands of ants that had appeared during the night and moved all the cans and cartons. But nobody listens to them.

The world's media responds within minutes, and social media is buzzing in every capital, every city, every village, with fascination about the contents, as well as a sense of anxiety and even fear.

Popular themes on social media included:

'Must be an elaborate hoax.'

'I think the leaders should agree to the demands.'

'We should just ignore this bullshit. Nothing will happen.'

'I believe it. We have killed too many creatures.'

'It's all rubbish, with letters created from rubbish. Slam dunk. I bet those drunks did it.'

A video clip of the last letters being formed, with no human involvement, goes viral, and soon causes some consternation:

'There's defo something weird going on.'

'They say it was them that took all those people years ago. Could be serious. Maybe they'll empty stadiums all over again.'

'I knew someone that disappeared 22 years ago. Never returned. No message. Nothing at all. It was terrible.'

'Why shouldn't the leaders give themselves up? It's us whose lives are threatened most.'

'You can do anything with cameras these days. Don't believe it!'

'The end of the world is knee high.'

'The end the world is the knight of Nee.'

'Bloody Trumbushton, he should go in that spaceship, or whatever it is, and the rest of them bastards.'

'Nobody should lift a finger till we know this is serious, and not some weirdo's prank.'

'"You barely scratched me, ha, ha. okay, we'll call it a

draw. Had enough eh? Come back here. I'll bite your legs off."'

'That's the knight of Nee, when armless and legless, and that will be Trumbushton calling out like an idiot if he ignores this message.'

'No way, the enemy will be the knight of Nee once we get at them.'

'Only thing is, if it's like 22 years ago, they won't be knights of Nee once we get at them. We'll be the ones looking the fools.'

US President Trumbushton speaks meanwhile to the ever-lasting Chinese Chairman Xi, European leaders, and the Indian President. Between them, they have spoken to other leaders on the list, from Africa, Latin America and Asia. They all agree with the US President that all affected countries will increase security for all the leaders to a maximum, and at the same time refuse to agree to the demands from the spaceship.

President Trumbushton also speaks to the President of Exxon Mobil, one of the business leaders, whose senior staff are coordinating a response from the global business leaders, with assistance from the President of Huawei in China, who is talking with Chinese business leaders. The President of Exxon Mobil confirms to President Trumbushton that the business leaders will follow the approach taken by the political leaders.

President Trumbushton also tasks the head of NASA and senior spooks from the CIA and DIA with tracing the spaceship, and, in NASA's case, gives them the task of assessing whether the spaceship can be attacked.

24 hours pass.

30 hours pass.

Messages are passed between those on the list

congratulating themselves on their steadfastness.

But then news comes from the office of the Australian Prime Minister. He has been attacked by flying ants while walking from his office to his car. They attack his neck and the inside of his mouth with poison, and although he is rushed to Canberra's main hospital, he dies en route, possibly from asphyxiation.

Social media goes wild with this news.

'The threat is real! Get those bastards in that spaceship.'

'Someone's up to something. Blaming some aliens. Some sly assassin.'

'It's the new Mata Hari. Bet you it's all a cunning plan to kill political leaders.'

'Get John Le Carré on it, he would know who is behind it.'

'Just a writer of stories, Le Carré, not a spook.'

'Isis I bet. Isis or Al Qaida. A bastardly dastardly plan to kill off political leaders and cause panic.'

'It may be an isolated incident. Just bad luck. A few rogue ants kill Aussie president. Let's not get carried away.'

'I say it's BOSS, or the CIA, or one of them. It's a conspiracy to get us all paranoid and bring in harsh laws.'

'What is this about insect extinction? Why is it linked to the Aussie Pressie?'

'I say kill all ants.'

'What good would that do? We don't even know if they are just being used for the murders. Must be someone behind them.'

'A zoologist maybe.'

'Entomologist, you mean, I think.'

'But must be one with murderous tendencies, or terrorist

leanings.'

    'ISIS then.'

    'No CIA, defo.'

    'No. Don't ignore this. The threat is real. Very real.'

Meanwhile, news starts coming out of mass deaths in Kerala, India, in Jakarta, Indonesia, in Mexico City, Naples, Italy and in Tokyo, Japan. The numbers in each case are thought to be in the tens of thousands, and in total 250,000 to 300,000, with first thoughts being that the water supply has been poisoned.

There are reports of mass funerals in Kerala and Indonesia, with hundreds of thousands taking part.

Initial tests suggest that the water has been poisoned by hemlock or fool's parsley.

Substantial straggly remnants of each are found by reservoirs at several of the cities affected.

The numbers keep rising, as other cities around the world report mass deaths, to the point where it is widely reported that at least 900,000 are now dead from the same type of water poisoning, and the numbers are still rising.

    'My bloody parents dead. Who the hell is doing this!?'

    'My sister, my two brothers, their children. All dead. The fuckers who did this.'

    'My mum, my aunt, my sister. All gone. They were just having their tea.'

    'It's happening all over. Thousands of deaths.'

    'Tens of thousands.'

    'If I find the buggers, I will kill the lot.'

    'There's talk of hemlock poisoning. In the water.'

    'Hemlock? What's effing hemlock?'

    'Used by people in ancient stories, I reckon.'

'Cleopatra, weren't it?'

'No, that was an asp.'

'Socrates then. Clever Greek bloke.'

'We could do with some clever Greek bloke today, to get to the bottom of this.'

'Lots of eco stuff in the message. Species being killed off and all that. Could be green nutters.'

'Green terrorists.'

'Could be some rich people who support green causes and can finance this shit.'

'Shut up guys. My whole family gone. I don't know what the hell I'm going to do. They were just sat having a bite to eat.'

'Someone's going to face hell for doing this.'

'You and whose army?'

'Something has to be done and quick.'

'I reckon only Richard Branson has the eco perspective, the money, and the madness, to do anything like this.'

'No way.'

'You're off your rocker.'

'Branson? I've just heard he's dead now too. Don't reckon it's him.'

The news now comes of a very elderly Richard Branson, semi-retired Chair of Virgin, being killed by poison ants shortly before midnight, while taking a nightcap at his expansive villa on Necker Island. There are widespread rumours, which dominate social media, that ants killed him by poisoning his penis.

The truth is stranger, according to Cindy, his personal assistant, who tweets that ants had created a pattern around his genitals, with meticulously made bite marks, forming the shape of a heart.

More social media hysteria follows:

'*Bloody Branson, killed by ants in his pants.*'

'*Formed a heart they reckon. Around his goolies.*'

'*No way!*'

'*Yes way! Ants make a heart. What do you make of that then?*'

'*Someone's got a sense of humour.*'

'*Pretty weird sense of humour, if you ask me. I'll fucking kill him.*'

'*He's dead already.*"

'*Is it real?*'

'*Duh! Yea! Doofbag.*'

'*I reckon it's the CIA. They hate Branson.*'

'*No, Isis-lookalike more like.*'

'*Didn't Branson threaten the US trade in spaceships carrying space tourists? Maybe someone wanted to kill him so they could get the market themselves.*'

'*Gibberish. That was years ago. Why the heart? Why the hemlock? The other people? Think about it.*'

'*Isis-lookalike makes the most sense.*'

'*They are not that bloody clever. They are just trying to copy ISIS.*'

'*Arabs have got killed too.*'

'*So, ISIS didn't kill Arabs?! Like hell they didn't.*'

'*Blame CIA, Mossad, Allah o Akhbar. Do not blame others.*'

'*Fuck off Moslem- lover.*'

'*Fuck off Moslem-hater.*'

'*I think it's a conspiracy by ants. Richard Branson — ants. Aussie Pressie — ants. Think about it.*'

143

'Put your brain back in, dopey, sleepy and grumpy. Like ants could do that. They may be clever little creatures, but not that bleeding clever.'

'Like fuck it's ants. Pull the other one, it's got bells on.'

'He may have a point. There's all those disappeared people 22 years ago. Never explained. The message says it's them. Then there's the signs of ants when Aussie President died, and now with Branson.'

'Yea, and there was the million killed the other day, with signs of hemlock, no perpetrator. Maybe whoever is doing it can control the ants, 'cos they are getting everywhere, all over the world. What organisation can do that?'

'CIA for one.'

'But all those deaths? Is that the CIA's style?'

'Why not? Throwing us all off the scent, I reckon.'

The death of Richard Branson kills off most rumours that Branson was behind the spaceship, but some think the spaceship had gone rogue, and that the rogue spaceman behind this turnabout had turned on the man (Branson) who had funded his mission.

There is far more tension amongst the world's politicians when the next message is discovered in Egypt within two hours of the news of Branson's killing.

In the middle of the night, a guard responsible for overseeing the Sphinx outside Cairo in Egypt goes out on to the sand for a piss.

He notices hundreds or perhaps thousands of ants not far from one of the sculpture's oversized paws. He thinks nothing of it, but when he and his colleagues come out to check around the magnificent sculpture in the morning, they see a very distinct Arabic message, written out in the sand using stones from the nearby desert, and covering the whole area in front of the beautifully formed front paws of the Sphinx.

The message is broadcast in English on social media in no time and goes viral. It reads:

This message is written with stones from the desert. The climate emergency is making the desert ever wider, ever deeper. Starvation is affecting many species, including millions of your people.

You have ignored our warning. If the leaders we have identified do not give themselves up to our spaceship within 24 hours Earth time, two political leaders will die and three business leaders will die. One million more people will die.

...

In the spaceship, Eleg now arranges to wake Souad and Abdul.

Souad is very groggy, as she comes through.

Eleg says: 'I am going to transport you both to the centre of Cairo.'

'We can get a taxi there without difficulty and find a hospital. Thanks,' says Abdul.

'Do you think you will manage?' asks Olga.

'They will ask awkward questions, but then nothing will be unusual for doctors in a Cairo hospital. I will blag my way to get a lift there.'

'You need to go to Tanzania as soon as you are better,' says Eleg.

'Tanzania?'

'Yes, the Serengeti in Tanzania. The surviving humans will go there. They will have a chance to live, taking up a new — and also very old — way of life in a new Braiby world.'

'OK. Sounds very interesting. But first we need to get to the hospital. Let's go.'

Eleg stations them on a polka dot-marked spot that has only now appeared and presses a few buttons near the door lift.

Shortly after, Souad and Abdul are no longer on the spaceship, and two strangers appear in the middle of a busy intersection in the centre of Cairo.

Fortunately, the traffic is at a standstill as a donkey and cart is blocking the way from two directions and moving very slowly. Fists are raised in the direction of the cart owner from all directions.

'I bet you are behind the Sphinx message,' says one.

'Yea, I reckon it is him,' shouts another, moving towards him.

'No, no, masters, please. I am just a donkey cart driver. I know nothing. Please.'

They let the donkey cart driver through. But fists are still raised and shaken at him by car drivers frustrated by the jam.

Slowly, painfully so, the traffic starts to move.

A bus comes by with a sign in Arabic saying 'hospital', and Souad signals the driver to stop. She helps Abdul on, where he sits on the floor. The person on the seat next to Souad has a mobile phone, with the screen message saying in Arabic: 'Panic after Sphinx warning to world leaders!'

Souad reads it with deep interest, thinking of Eleg. 'Could only be Eleg,' she thinks.

…

Within an hour of the Sphinx message appearing on social media, there is international videoconferencing involving almost all the political leaders, while business leaders come to a more ad hoc arrangement to communicate.

The discussion by the politicians focusses primarily on security.

US President Trumbushton announces:

'Arrangements are being made for me to go into the White House bunker (the presidential Emergency Operations Centre) under the East Wing. I have to remain alive until a solution can be found to this alleged threat.'

The UK Prime Minister also confirms that steps are being taken for her to enter the bunker that has been put in place for nuclear war.

Trumbushton reports: 'NASA reports to me that it can find no trace of the spaceship.'

President Xi says: 'We have also been unable to trace a spaceship. However, I can report that some hitherto unknown signals have been detected in airspace, and our best people have been working through the night to make sense of these, and to find evidence of the source and destination.'

Trumbushton says that NASA had also reported evidence of strange new signals. 'They suspect the Russians,' he says.

'We Russians have nothing to do with any of this,' shouts President Putin, now with a large paunch and barely any grey hair, 'I am as much at risk as the rest of you, and am taking my own steps for security.'

The French and Spanish presidents ask about the ants reported as having been seen at the Sphinx, and the ants involved in the deaths of the Australian President and Richard Branson. They also note the questions being asked about the mass poisoning of around a million people, mostly with hemlock, and that there were signs of ants around the remnants of the hemlock.

'Could ants have been involved in this?' asks the French President.

'The evidence is mounting that they are,' says the Spanish President.

They suggest that active steps should be taken to see if ants are somehow involved in the threats, or at least the implementation of the threats.

President Xi suggests that the French and Spanish leaders could look into this themselves, while the rest will focus on security.

The majority view is that nobody is to give themselves up to this new enemy by offering themselves to the alleged spaceship, which has still not been identified as present in the airspace around Planet Earth.

Only one political leader, the Indian President, says he would be happy to give himself up. He says: 'We cannot continue to let so many people die like this.'

'Yes, we can,' says the Russian President.

'When did we ever do different?' asks the US President Trumbushton.

'Speak for yourself,' says the Spanish President. 'You let climate change kill millions, now you let others die in their millions.'

'Climate change is natural world climate adjustment,' says Trumbushton, as a mosquito flies in, lands on his neck, and draws blood. 'What the fuck!' he shouts, as he slaps it, too late.

The business leaders take the same view as the majority of the political leaders, focussing on security.

The funeral of the Australian Prime Minister is set to take

place in four days' time. Unusually, no world leaders will be taking part, only their underlings, and the odd royal.

The word is that security is the paramount consideration, and that the threat facing world leaders is unusually high.

Operation Protect and Survive is the official name of the American response.

...

In Rome, the Italian President meets her head of security, Signor Bonetti. Bonetti explains that she will no longer carry out her normal activities, although public notices on the internet and elsewhere will give the impression that she is carrying out all her usual functions, with dates and venues given.

In fact, the President will be installed in a secret high-security building, which will include her accommodation during this period of high-level security. Bonetti also explains that he will be responsible for all security protocols in this special building.

For nearly 24 hours, all proceeds smoothly. When the President visits the toilet in the morning, though, all is not as it seems.

She notices powerful itching while sitting on the toilet. When she wipes the itching with toilet paper, ants start climbing up her arms. In no time, the ants are all over her body. She screams as loudly and shrilly as she can, and security people come to the toilet. But it is locked from the inside.

She tries to reach towards the door but, before she can, the ants have climbed into her mouth and bitten at her neck and injected poison and she is paralysed and unable to breathe. She cannot reach the lock of the door.

She tries to scream but it does not come out, as she slides to the floor. The ants all head back down into the toilet.

In the next 60 seconds, the security people break the door down to find the President on the floor. Bonetti makes an urgent call for medical aid, shouting down the phone:

'The President may only have moments left to live! Send the most senior doctor in Rome and support staff this minute.'

Meanwhile, a security woman tries to administer CPR, but there is no change. She says there is no pulse. The medical team arrive moments later, but they promptly declare the President to be dead.

There is no ant in sight.

...

In Brasilia, the Brazilian President is eating breakfast on the patio of his presidential palace. Around him are members of the National Guard, and there is a crack unit in front of the entrance to the palace, and snipers on the roof and at adjoining high points all around the building.

The President is about to put a tostada in his mouth when he sees an ant on it. As he tries to brush it off, a dozen land on his hand, a dozen more on the tostada, and in no time a few dozen on his lips, and in his eyes, his ears and throughout his hair.

He calls out, screaming at the top of his voice.

The guards run towards him as the President collapses. One calls an ambulance immediately as well as the head of security. The latter contacts the medical team who are stationed at the front of the palace.

The head of security unlocks the doors and they rush through to the patio to find the President fighting for his life, with his body stretched out on the patio and convulsing. The ants have gone, but there are bite marks all over his neck and on his lips. His eyes are bloodshot.

As the doctor seeks to resuscitate him, it is clear to her that the President is not responding at all, and there is barely a pulse. A helicopter lands with specialist medical personnel. They place a strap under the President and lift him into the helicopter, from where he is whisked off to the best hospital in Brasilia. However, with an hour, it is announced that the President is dead.

...

A limousine with blacked out windows is coasting along the A4 towards the GlaxoSmithKline headquarters at Brentford on the edge of London. The CEO is just checking documents that have come through by email for a meeting with directors that afternoon.

The driver shouts, 'Mama Mia, what is happening!'

After flicking on his warning lights, he pulls over with his windscreen smothered with millions of midges, many squished on the windscreen. His windscreen wipers cannot move, and the water squirters seem not to work. He opens the door with rag in hand.

Immediately, a swarm of flying ants enters the car and surrounds the head of the CEO. The driver gets straight on his mobile and calls first for medical aid from the HQ, and also the police. He grabs a towel from the passenger seat and tries to thwack the ants, but there are too many.

When the paramedics arrive, they find the CEO is dead.

The driver is unscathed. He says the flying ants simply flew off having stung the CEO on his neck, mouth, eyes and nose, and did not touch the driver.

…

The Amazon office of ageing CEO Jeff Bezos and his PA is in an extra-large drone that has been converted for this purpose to station itself in view of Golden Gate Bridge and the Californian coastline nearby. Bezos flies down in a man-sized drone each day for a lunch meeting with senior colleagues.

Bezos is eating his lunch of sushi dishes and a green salad in a large glass domed dining hall. On the salad, as he begins to slice a piece of lettuce with his knife, eggs start to hatch, and tiny white, almost translucent creatures emerge. Probably ants, he thinks, his face reddening at anger that this could be happening.

He shouts down his phone for the catering manager, Ramos, to come immediately.

'Immediately!' he screams.

Some of the ants start flying, they buzz round the CEO's head and head towards his mouth. He flaps his hands, asking where the hell is the catering manager, until his voice is cut off by ants in his throat.

His financial director Jim calls the medical centre with phone in one hand and tries with the other to flap at the ants too with paper napkins and a plate. To no avail.

As Ramos begins to stride across the dining hall, Bezos collapses on the floor, his head covered with ants. Jim tries to lift him by the shoulder, with Ramos taking the other shoulder as he reaches him. Both the mouth and nose of Bezos are full of these tiny ants.

As he spots the paramedics arriving outside, Ramos calls out for someone with CPR expertise. A colleague, Spinelli, runs over and tries to resuscitate him, while Ramos tries to remove the ants from his mouth and nose. There is no sign of Bezos breathing.

As paramedics arrive in the dining hall, Spinelli announces that there is no pulse. Shortly after, the paramedics confirm the same. They surmise from his colouring and the location of ants inside his throat that he has died from asphyxiation.

...

Another corporate leader death occurs when the CEO of General Motors asks his driver to stop for a hamburger as they travel by car into downtown Detroit. As the car door opens, flying ants get into the car and engulf the throat and nose of the CEO before he can get help. He dies of asphyxiation.

...

During the same day, reports come of mass deaths in Bombay, Cairo, Chicago, Florence, Vienna, Kiev, Jalalabad, Shanghai, Cochin, Cape Town and elsewhere.

Early estimates suggested that around a million have died altogether in incidents that are remarkably similar to the incidents 2-3 days previously.

Hemlock is again believed to be the poison used. This is confirmed later in the day, with analysis coming from each of the cities where so many had died the previous day, indicating strongly that it was hemlock.

Social media is more varied in tone and content than before:

'Has to be the CIA as it is so global, I say.'

'Has to be copycat or lookalike ISIS as it is so global.'

'Not copycat ISIS. Mossad. With Russian help.'

'Could be a superbreed of ants, with special powers. Their first message said they abducted those million people. Why not these?'

'Yea, of course, or a superbreed of lizards. What was that film?'

'Godzilla, maybe.'

'Gargantua? Is that what you are thinking of?'

'Wrong films, I think. More like Planet of the Apes. Maybe that's it.'

'Like Planet of the Apes is real, and the apes have come to protect creatures here!'

'Why not? We can't be the only living beings in the universe.'

'All this movie rubbish. This is real. Real people killing real people. Millions.'

'With an environmentalist agenda.'

'Agenda. Wassat?'

'A plan. A green plan, to change our planet.'

'Or is that just a trick? A deception?'

'They must be very powerful people. They get everywhere.'

'And what of all those people abducted 20 years ago? Are they linked?'

'22 years ago. About 300,000 of them.'

'*Christ, was it that long ago? Don't believe it.*'

'*Maybe all 300,000 have been brainwashed and they've come back to wreak their havoc on earth.*'

'*Orson Welles couldn't make this up.*'

'*More like H G Wells.*'

'*C'mon guys, millions are dying. There must be better ideas about who did it. And why.*'

'*Must be ecological, that's a thread running through the messages.*'

'*Must be mega powerful, with loads of people to help.*'

'*Maybe it's schoolchildren. Remember that Greta Thunberg Swedish kid all these years ago. Now a mega politico. Tried at that time to change a whole generation.*'

'*You're off your rocker. These are serious people. Psychopaths even. Kill randomly. That's not Greta.*'

'*They kill millions randomly.*'

'*Damned right.*'

....

The next message to the world leaders, on Brisbane Beach, early morning, with coral from the reef, is spotted by a pair of early morning surfers.

Coral is a vital part of the ecosystem. It sustains much sea life, which in turn sustains much bird life and much life on the land. Your cavalier attitude to the climate is destroying much of the earth's coral.

You continue to ignore our warnings. With your selfishness, and your individual approach, you are putting your whole species at risk. This is symbolic. It is what you have been doing for so many generations. But it is worse, because

155

you have put other species at risk, too many, including ours.

Now, three political leaders will be killed, and six business leaders, if you do not agree to our demands within 24 hours, Earth time.

When the political leaders meet holographically through satellite link around an hour after the message goes viral, there is not the sense of unity experienced by most at the previous meeting.

Many are supportive of the Indian President now, with two million people now dead, three political leaders dying regardless of all the security, and several CEOs of major corporations dying in terrible circumstances.

Trumbushton, the US President, and the Chinese President Xi Jin Ping, are resolutely in favour of tightening security further and renewing efforts to trace the spaceship.

President Xi reports that his specialists' analysis backs up the concerns raised two days before by the Spanish and French leaders.

'They have concluded that ants seem to be behind most of the deaths,' he says, 'as examination of the remains of the hemlock plants in different cities, at strategic water supply points, suggests there were ant trails in different directions from the places where the hemlock was found. The role of ants in the deaths of many political and business leaders is also noted by these analysts.'

'This is exactly what we suspected. We must take appropriate action,' says the French President.

'Further,' says President Xi, 'a specialist team based in Chengdu is examining how ants can be destroyed in large numbers, by targeting them in key locations with pesticides. They expect to report in 48 hours.'

Trumbushton says that the State Department has tasked a panel of experts from around the country to explore how to take on ants at a mass level, strategically. They had asked for a week, but they had been told they have at most 72 hours to produce a full report.

But half the remaining political leaders now wish to agree to the demand to go to the spaceship. And two thirds of the business leaders want this.

There is a stand-up row for part of the meeting.

The Indian President says:

'I am asked to say this on behalf of many of our colleagues, and I say it also on my behalf. Mr Trumbushton and President Xi, the die is cast. Are you going to continue to sacrifice humankind to seek to spare yourselves?'

'It is a vain and empty threat,' says Trumbushton.

'We do not know the enemy yet,' adds Xi, 'so this complicates our decision.'

'But we know that millions have died, and that they have the ability to track down senior people in politics and business and kill them,' says the Indian President, 'this is hardly an empty threat.'

'They claim to have a spaceship, but there is no physical evidence of that. We know ants cannot organise all these things, although they are certainly involved at the business end of the killing. I am the US President. I am not giving myself up to something or to someone I do not know and do not comprehend.'

'You put your own selfish interests first, that is the be all and end all of it!' counters the South African President, his face almost beetroot with anger. And many nod their heads in agreement.

'They talk of their species being under threat,' says the Spanish President. 'We know how much ants are involved. We have to believe that there is another planet with more intelligent ants, able to travel in space, and able to talk to ants on Earth. This is surely a better explanation for the messages, and for what has happened.'

'I agree,' says the French President. 'We can only speculate, but my colleague's hypothesis is consistent with the evidence that we have. Enough is enough. The world has had enough. It is time for the leaders of the USA and China to agree to talk to our enemy and try to spare further mass deaths.'

President Trumbushton looks at President Xi, who nods.

'Give us 48 hours,' says Trumbushton. 'We will give you a response then.'

'I agree,' says Xi, 'we will respond in two days.'

...

The next morning, the Spanish Prime Minister undresses in his private bathroom and steps into the shower. As he adjusts the knob to his ideal water temperature, it is not water that emerges but countless ants, some flying around his head, confusing him, and others taking advantage of his confusion to crawl through and over his hair, down to his neck, and into his nose and mouth. As they start to enter his mouth, he tries to call out, but his call is reduced in volume by his fear of the ants all over his head, and it emerges as a weak shriek.

Within half an hour, he dies from asphyxiation. It takes twice as long before anyone realises what has happened.

...

The Indonesian President dies in the bathing pool adjacent to his sleeping quarters, which are inside a highly guarded presidential building, when he is entranced by the bridge formed by ants across the bathing pool, before they fly up and attack his mouth and nose in great numbers. The guards are too slow to realise the danger, and respond too late to save the President, and the ants fly off as soon as the President ceases to breathe.

...

The Pakistani PM is holding a special meeting with ministers in his cabinet office. Security is tight, with several layers of guards all around the building and drones and guards heavily policing all surrounding roads. The PM and his fellow ministers are unaware that the beautifully woven and textured designed carpet that covers much of the floor is not quite what it seems.

The pattern of the carpet is beginning to move.

The dark grey and pink elements of the carpet pattern are ants, and they are moving towards the chair of the Prime Minister.

Nobody notices as the ants climb up the back legs of the chair, and then its back and over the top, and then start descending, right by the neck of the Prime Minister.

Thwack The Prime Minister slaps his neck, and he is surprised to find a bloody squashed ant in the palm of his hand, but even as he inspects his hand, there are suddenly painful bites all round his neck.

A hush descends for a moment all around as ants appear

from the Prime Minister's hair and climb down his face and into his nose and mouth.

One minister immediately starts ringing the emergency number on his mobile, while three others rush to try to sweep the ants from the Prime Minister's face, and two others rush to the door to the room, calling for urgent assistance from security outside.

The Prime Minister, meanwhile, is paralysed from the ant poison in his neck, and is unable to move. Ants have climbed inside his mouth and nose, and the ministers fear that they could do more damage by trying to extricate them before specialists arrive.

But by the time a doctor arrives, just moments later, she can find no pulse, and considers there is no prospect of resuscitation. She says that the pallor on the Prime Minister's face suggests asphyxiation. There are also signs his heart has stopped, she adds.

...

In the USA, six CEOs, two of them heads of oil companies, two heads of car-making companies, and two heads of IT companies, are meeting in a mountain retreat in Colorado, having travelled in secret from different parts of the USA, and driven up in six all electric limos with blacked out windows from Denver airport. They discuss the current threats to them and other corporate and political leaders. They are unanimous in backing the position of the US President.

They are unaware of the ants with unusually strong mandibles that have congregated near the six limousines and are chewing their way through brake cables on each limousine, while the CEOs are chewing their way through blood-dripping rib eye steak.

A report on social media the next morning goes viral. It tells of six limousines flying off the mountain top at the first sharp bend in the road, leading to the deaths of six chauffeurs but also, and more significantly, six of the leading corporate CEOs in the USA.

A week later, the police have no clue as to who may have tampered with the brakes of the CEOs' limousines. There was no evidence on CCTV footage of any person coming near the limos at any time while the CEOs were inside the hotel. Further, interviews with the few dozen employees and family members of the CEOs who knew their whereabouts did not reveal any possible culprits. The ants left no clues.

...

Over the next 24 hours, there are reports of around a million dying in a number of cities, including Bogota (Colombia), New Orleans, Ottawa, Sydney (Australia), Yangon (formerly Rangoon, Burma), Hanoi, Lagos (Nigeria), Hiroshima (Japan), Montevideo (Uruguay), Glasgow, Frankfurt and Wellington (New Zealand).

As previously, straggling pieces of hemlock are found near the main sources of water for each city.

Around 30 hours after the deaths of the six CEOs, the head of security of the Bernabeu stadium in Madrid, Spain notices something strange when he enters the stadium early in the morning. There is unusual colouring on the otherwise pristine green football pitch. As he approaches, he stops in his tracks quite abruptly. Shocked. There are hundreds or even thousands of dead bees covering the central area of the pitch. The bees form letters that give the following message in Spanish:

Bees pollinate the majority of your crops. They provide honey. They are a vital part of the ecosystem. You humans will make bees extinct because of the destructive way your species live. In the last year, 100,000 species have been made extinct. If you do not now meet our demands, it may be the time for your species to face extinction.

You have 24 hours, human time, to agree to our demands. If you do not, six political leaders will die, 12 business leaders will die, and one million other people will die…

At 7:30 am, Spanish time, images of the message go out on social media, and soon go viral.

There is now turmoil when the political leaders communicate by satellite link.

Only the US and Chinese Presidents, and the Austrian leader, wish to stand firm.

'Give us 12 more hours,' says President Trumbushton. President Xi nods.

The other political leaders insist that there will soon be almost none of them left, and that too many millions have died, and keep dying.

It is evident from US officials advising the meeting that no progress has been made in taking on the ants, apart from concerted but random attacks on ant heaps, and no progress has been made in identifying the enemy that is using the ants to kill.

Business leaders are now unanimously in favour of giving in to the demands of the spaceship.

The US President advises that military helicopters and drones have attacked about two thousand ant heaps, killing hundreds of millions of ants.

The Indian President asks whether it was not true that all the soldiers in the military helicopters have died when thousands of flying ants got into their engines and forced the helicopters to crash.

The US President confirms this. 'Small price to pay,' he says, 'if it stops some of this senseless killing. But our hearts go out to the relatives of those brave men who gave up their lives.'

There are mass demonstrations against the political leaders in towns and cities throughout the world. Workplaces close down, schools close and city transport systems come to a halt as people occupy town and city centres in unprecedented numbers. In some European countries, governments cease to function as so many employees are on strike and so many buildings are occupied.

The mass media across the industrialised world, with only a few exceptions, are demanding that the political leaders must give themselves up.

After the meeting with other leaders, the US President returns to the bunker under the White House. The Chinese President goes to his palace in the heart of the Forbidden City in Beijing, surrounded by several layers of security.

President Trumbashton starts itching uncontrollably. His Chief of Staff asks what the problem is.

The President says his suit is itching ferociously. The Chief of Staff inspects it and spots tiny flies emerging from larvae all throughout his suit, on the inside of the fabric in particular. He advises that they need to head out fast and find a different location, as the bunker seems to have become infested. The President agrees.

The moment they emerge from the bunker to head straight into the presidential limousine, President Trumbushton disappears.

His security detail and chief advisers look around dumbfounded.

The President is nowhere to be seen. His head of security immediately orders a red alert, and contacts the heads of the CIA, DIA, the Air Force and the Army to arrange an emergency meeting within an hour. He also orders for the White House to be emptied, and for it to be locked up and fully guarded militarily until further notice.

...

What happens in Beijing mirrors what happened in Washington. President Xi Jin Ping simply disappears. His chief security officer orders that the Forbidden City is emptied, and a guard is to be put in place to ensure nobody can enter. The whole of Beijing to be placed on high alert.

....

Hospital in Cairo

'Abdul.'

'Yes.' The room is white and clinical, with a fading photograph of former President Nasser on one wall.

The doctor leans towards Abdul. The conversation is in Arabic.

'I will not ask you to explain how you lost your penis. What is clear is that you have suffered a violent attack, which has left substantial bruising, aside from the terrible loss of your penis.'

'Is there any risk of infection, or anything that I should worry about?' asks Abdul.

'We have cleaned up the wound, and this should slowly heal. You've been here a few days now for checks and I think you can now be discharged. In terms of your psychological reaction to your physical loss, I can recommend someone if you wish, but you will need to pay privately.'

'I will not need this, thank you.'

'The wound to your rectum is more superficial and should heal more quickly. You can expect to be uncomfortable passing stools for several days.'

'Tell me about it!'

'I will not charge you, given your circumstances. I wish you well.'

'Thank you.'

Abdul leaves, and finds his way gingerly to the genito-urinary ward for women, which means going down various corridors, negotiating past any numbers of ill and injured people squatting on floors, sleeping, or searching for where to go. In a few places, people seem to have lost their lives where they sit and are slumped over.

'Souad!' he calls at last, as he comes into the ward. 'What's the news?'

'Not pregnant, thank heavens. How are you?' she asks. 'I've been worried about you.'

'I can't really talk about it. It's still very traumatic for me. But the doctor says that I am on the road to recovery physically. What about your other wounds, your rectum?'

'Not great, but slowly healing, like yours. Let's go, shall

we? You said on the way here you may want to look for your mother and your brother Mohammed.'

'Yes, I know the way. I've walked from the city centre umpteen times before. Let's just take it nice and slow.'

They find the exit to the hospital and head on their way, through a maze of narrow streets. The streets are much emptier than Abdul remembered, and there are a number of instances where they find themselves stepping over corpses.

As they reach the edge of the city, the Great Pyramid of Giza is over to their left. Tourists are still visible all over its structure, looking tiny like ants, thinks Souad, as she then becomes aware of the irony, having seen such large ants on Howl.

They are now on simple sandy paths, recognisable only by having fewer weeds than the scrubland and semi-desert to the side.

They eventually approach the settlement where Abdul's mother Fatima lived. There is no sign of her.

Abdul inspects the simple lean-to where they had lived and casts his gaze across the field where they grew crops. Nothing. He looks at Souad and holds his hands out open-faced to suggest that the cupboard seems bare.

'I need a rest,' says Abdul. 'I will light the stove and put some water on. Sit here if you like,' and he beckons her to sit on a wooden stool that his mother always used.

As he heads to a nearby stream for water, he hears a scratching sound nearby. He turns to look, and sees a mat of banana leaves move, as well as an old door that the leaves were camouflaging.

Mohammed's face slowly emerges from under the door, and his eyes show pleasant surprise.

'Mohammed, brother!' and Abdul embraces him as he climbs out.

'Abdul, what a surprise!' and everything is so strange here. 'But look, there is another person wants to meet you too, but you need to help me.'

And Abdul pulls the door fully away from the hole, and climbs back in. Carefully, he lifts Fatima up for Abdul to take her.

'Mother! Am I pleased to meet you!'

'My son! I feared I would never see you again! Hold me tight. Hold me really tight, dear Abdul.' And she wrapped her arms around him as if she would never let him go.

'Harrumph,' comes a plaintive interjection from the direction of Souad.

Abdul quickly turns his head her way, and smiles. 'Mother, Mohammed, this is Souad, a refugee from Iraq, who has accompanied me here.'

'*Salaam Alekom.*' say Mohammed and Fatima in unison, welcoming her by extending their arms.

They squat on the ground near the lean-to. Abdul pours some tea, which is now made.

'I have some news for you, Abdul, and it's going to be hard for you to hear,' says Fatima.

Abdul looks at her, and notices Mohammed looking very serious, and nodding at Abdul to listen to his mother.

'I am dying,' says Fatima. 'I am becoming paralysed slowly, and we have seen this with many neighbours. Death follows quite soon.'

'It's true, Abdul,' says Mohammed. 'I dug the hole for us to try and protect us from this plague, but we had to come out for water. Slowly, many of us are dying. You and Souad should not stay here any longer. It is not safe.'

'I will stay with mother. It is so long since I last saw her, and I cannot leave her at this time.'

'I will stay too,' says Souad.

'You are too pig-headed for your own good,' says Fatima. 'But at least stay in the hole with Mohammed. You may have a chance of surviving, as Mohammed has not yet succumbed.'

'OK. Let us have some bread now, and rest soon,' replies Abdul. 'I will tell you my news all in good time.'

In the morning, Abdul emerges from the hole to find his mother has died in the night. He tugs on Mohammed's hair to stir him, and they prepare her body for burial.

Souad wakes also and makes some tea. They hold a brief service and use the hole, which is about a body length long, as her grave. Abdul and Mohammed fill the grave, and again say prayers when they are done. Abdul explains what happened to him and Souad for the rest of the morning. Mohammed stops him as he is talking about the rape, and holds him tight for several long minutes, sobbing profusely.

They then decide to leave, and soon head off to the Nile. En route, Abdul explains to Mohammed about the need to travel to Tanzania and gives him fuller details of life on Howl and on the spaceship, with Souad adding in a few details in between times.

The scene at the bank of the Nile is chaotic. Hundreds of people are fighting over a few dozen boats. There is ferocious bargaining over payment. Fists fly.

Cruise ships are overfull with hundreds more than they should carry. Several people dangling on the deck rails can be seen falling into the river. The distinct look of crocodile eyes can be seen approaching, and soon there are splashes and waves as a struggle ensues between an unfortunate fallen passenger and a crocodile or two.

Abdul suggests they walk upstream a few kilometres. Eventually, after collecting dates and bananas from palms they pass, they find a small boat where the occupants have died. The three of them lift the bodies out and let them float away. They then climb aboard and start gently rowing upstream.

....

Spaceship

Trumbushton is slightly drowsy but recovers his senses to the sight of a strange cavernous metallic structure with a few robots that seem to be immense robotic versions of ants.

There is also a young dusky-coloured woman, and young black man, neither of whom he recognises.

His first reaction is to be struck dumb.

The Chinese President comes to also and is dumbstruck as he casts his eyes around him.

President Trumbushton blusters:

'Who the hell are you? What right do you and your weird robots have to hold me here? I will order the National Guard to take you all on, and if necessary, bring the whole might of our Air Force against you. They will hunt you down wherever we are.'

Olga responds: 'I should sit down if I were you. You will be here for a while.'

Trumbushton looks daggers at her: 'Who the fuck do you think you are, addressing the President of the United States like that?'

Xi stands impassive, casts his eyes again at the robot ants, and at Olga and Johann in turn.

'You are nothing,' said Olga, 'both of you. Without all your team of personnel, your armed forces, your imposing buildings, you are just flesh and blood.'

'I will not speak to you. I will only speak to a leader, to someone of my rank.'

'You have no choice,' states Johann, trying to explain. 'The ant species does not have leaders. They have a collective brain, so that a million ants can think as one. It's a wonderful thing to behold, and I have learnt that it is something of genius, with extraordinary advantages over the individual thinking that is characteristic of humans.'

'Well I can tell you, upstart, that I, for one, think individually, not collectively, as you call it. America could not be run in any other way. And I tell you that everything you say is bunkum and claptrap. There are four letter words — plenty of four-letter words — that say it better, but I do not intend to stoop so low with such garbage as you two represent. The fact is, I am a president, you are Mr and Mrs Nobody or, if you prefer, Mr and Mrs Insignificant, and I will not deal with you.'

'That is fine,' says Olga. 'But until you change your mind, you will not receive water or food, and you will sit here until you die. Meanwhile, most of the human race will be in the process of dying out, as you will not have taken the steps that can help to prevent this.'

'Let me have a quiet word with President Trumbushton,' says President Xi. He speaks in Mandarin Chinese, and Eleg translates this for Olga and Johann.

Xi speaks to Trumbushton in English. 'We have no option, esteemed President. We are leaders of two great nations. Our people depend on us to talk to these people, even though they are lowly people, with no leadership position. If we do nothing, the people for whom we have responsibility may be wiped out. These people and the ant robots have shown their power to kill very large numbers of people. Equally, I believe that it is possible that this is a ruse, a trick, and there is no such threat, but neither you nor I can take this risk.'

'I don't like it,' said Trumbushton, 'I don't like it one bit. We can defeat these pathetic Nobody people, their creature friends, and their robots.'

'I think it is just us two, in this strange space, against foes who have the upper hand.'

'I give off a secret signal,' says Trump. 'My people will find me, and soon.'

'I have an implanted device, also,' responds Xi. 'But neither we nor you Americans could locate their spaceship, so perhaps our signals are blocked. We found some unexplained signals, it is true, but we could not pinpoint a craft, this craft. We are, for once, powerless.'

'Might just be a mock-up, President Jee. I've never seen a spaceship anything like this.'

'I fear, like me, that you have not seen an alien spaceship before.'

'They don't impress me. The robots, these two Nobody's. It's a sham.'

'It is the only explanation, esteemed President, for all the deaths, all the massacres of so many people, the messages, the unusual use of coral, bees etc.'

'There must be another explanation.'

'Do you play poker, esteemed President?'

'I certainly do.'

'They hold all the aces, honourable President, we seem to hold no cards, except perhaps jokers.'

'Goddammit. For the sake of my people, I will humour these impudent insulting folks for a few minutes.'

'I am grateful, esteemed colleague,' says Xi.

Trumbushton turns to face Olga and Johann.

'What do you expect from us, what demands, Mr and Mrs Nobody? And under what right do you detain here such eminent personages as myself and my esteemed colleague President Jee?' he asks.

'We represent a species that is far greater, and far older, than the human species. This species can destroy human life on earth, if that is your choice,' replies Johann. 'By refusing our demands, you have brought the extinction of the human race much nearer. But there is one last chance for you.'

'Utter balderdash, poppycock!' shouts Trumbushton, 'you and whose army — these poxy robots here? You think you can bring me here and threaten me like this? In no time, US planes will be coming to get me out of here!'

Eleg lifts a finger and fires a white sticky substance at the President's right foot.

'Shit! What is this? Can't move my damned foot. What kind of stuff is that?'

'Eleg, our robot friend, can disable each of you bit by bit, until you only have your mouth free to speak, if you continue to refuse to talk,' explains Olga.

'My Air Force will only be seconds away, or minutes. Just you see,' shouts Trumbushton.

Eleg lifts a finger and fires the same sticky white substance at the President's left foot.

'Damn you, pesky good for nothing robot. I won't have

this. I simply will not be treated like this as the President of the United States.'

'Then talk. Are you going to continue to jeopardise the future of the human race by refusing to cooperate? Is your selfishness, egotism and pig-headedness so deep-rooted that the lives of billions of people count for nothing?' asks Johann.

'What are you asking of us?' asks Xi.

'Our masters want you to return to Earth, with our help, and order the end of oil, coal and gas production, industrial production and plane, ship and train travel in your home countries, and return your two countries to pastoral economies within ten years,' says Olga. 'It is expected that petrol and diesel cars will soon run out of fuel if you agree to our demands.'

'Right, so a couple of Nobody's and a handful of ham joke robots want us to bring an end to the prosperity of our countries, on your say so. You can kiss my ass,' says Trumbushton.

Eleg lifts a finger.

'No, don't do that, Robot, just don't... I take the "ham" bit back. Seriously.'

But Eleg fires the sticky white stuff at the President's right hand, which is now paralysed.

'Damn, fuck and blast you, Robot!' screams Trumbushton.

. . . . .

Abdul, Mohammed and Souad on the Nile

'We need more provisions,' says Souad.

'I can see some date palms ahead; we can perhaps find a spot on the bank where we can pull in and moor the boat briefly,' responds Abdul.

'There is a boat there, and some more people,' says Souad, looking around. 'Seems to be another hearse full of the dead, like so many we have seen, sadly.'

'One of them just moved slightly,' says Abdul, 'let's try to pull alongside it.'

A woman is slumped in the lap of an older woman, who seems to be consoling her with her palm. Their black hair is just visible under their chadors.

As they come alongside, Souad reaches over: 'Is she dying?' she asks.

'She does not have long, as she cannot breathe. I myself may only last a day longer,' replies the woman.

Abdul and Mohammed step out of the boat on to the bank and find some twine to tie it at the bankside, next to the other boat.

'My name is Souad. Is there anything I can do?'

There is flicker of activity in the dying woman's eyes, and she turns her face slowly towards Souad.

'Ashraf! I cannot believe it is you! I thought I would never see you again,' says Souad, tears flooding out.

'Souad,' she whispers, her brow wrinkled with pain as she does so, and Souad reaches over and caresses her head.

'I am her friend,' says the woman, 'I am called Mina, and I'm from Kuwait. You must be her sister, dear Souad. She has said so much about you. We have travelled from my homeland. Trying to reach Tanzania. But we had some bread and humus yesterday. We were so desperately hungry we took the risk. Now we seem to be dying like everyone else.'

'I am mortified that I've found you, amongst all these dying people, but that you have so little time.' Souad stares at Ashraf mournfully.

She holds her sister and is silent for a few moments. Then she turns to Mina:

'I am grateful to you, Mina, for being with Ashraf through this difficult time. I am so grateful that she has not been alone.'

Abdul and Mohammed arrive with some dates and bananas, freshly plucked.

'Abdul, Mohammed, I wish to stay with Ashraf,' she says.

'Of course,' says Abdul.

They stay silent as Souad and Mina share in holding Ashraf. Starlight provides a half-light as the sun drops below the horizon, so that only body shapes are visible, and the profile of a face. The water shimmers seductively by the riverbank, lapping gently, and there are crickets also to interrupt the silence, with the birds now at rest.

Ashraf's eyes close for the final time that night, and they prepare to bury her as the sun rises. Souad reaches inside her top, where a tiny flask of perfume is held in a simple threaded pocket. She dots a little perfume on Ashraf's body, and fashions what she can of a shroud from Ashraf's undergarment to cover her body.

Souad prays to herself. Two boats pass, and the occupants lower their heads out of respect.

Souad is silent all the next day, except for muffled crying.

Mohammed suggests that they stay together from here, and that they use Mina's boat, as it is a better boat. Mina agrees, and the others climb aboard. Suddenly, Abdul points at something moving in the water. Like two hooded eyes.

'A crocodile,' says Mina. 'I have seen several. Locals say

175

they have come further north than normal because there is less of a threat from human guns, and also there is so much food. They are not thought to be dangerous to the living as they are gorging themselves on the dead.'

Nervously, they watch as the crocodile slides past them and heads to the bank where the other boat is moored. They ease their boat a little further into the river.

A grey bird with a long white throat flies towards the crocodile.

Souad and Mina start as the crocodile opens its mouth wide, a fearsome set of dentures showing, only for the bird to climb inside the mouth and start pecking at its teeth.

'I've heard of this,' says Mohammed, 'the bird is a plover and it cleans the bits that are stuck between the crocodile's teeth. It provides welcome food for the plover, and for the crocodile it means that the bits of meat stuck there do not go fetid and make it ill.'

'What is that shiny thing, like a jewel, towards the back of its teeth?' asks Souad, both dumbstruck and very wary.

'It looks like it may be an earring, or a finger ring,' suggests Mina,

'It must have come off some poor person as they were swallowed by this brute,' says Abdul.

'Yuk. I've had enough,' says Mohammed, 'we can't recover the ring. I'm going to steer us away.'

'But what if I dived in…' wonders Abdul aloud.

'No way, no way, not for an Allah-forsaken ring,' says Mohammed.

And they row off.

Mina dies the next night, and they bury her at the bankside too, again with a few dots of perfume after cleansing her body and fashioning a makeshift shroud.

Washington, USA

Back in the Pentagon, confusion reigns.

They have a bleeper inserted next to President's larynx, in order to keep track wherever he is, but they cannot trace him.

Eventually, they track the direction he went in from two different angles and put a whole crack team on the task of seeking to identify where he may have gone.

They still do not find out where the President is.

...

The Spaceship

President Xi asks of Olga and Johann: 'These are difficult things that you ask of a political leader. Do you have other demands?'

'We also want you to make immediate connection with political leaders throughout Planet Earth,' says Johann. 'You will inform them that the future of the human species requires an end to current oil, gas and coal production, industrial production and mechanised travel — aircraft, ships, trains and commercial trucks. They are also, like your countries, to return human society to a pastoral existence within ten years.'

'Billions will die of starvation in just a few years if we do this,' says Xi.

'A trillion ants, trillions of other insects, and hundreds of thousands of animals,' explains Olga, 'have died in recent times at the hands of humans, destabilising the earth's eco system, and putting life on the planet at risk. We are putting forward a proposal that will allow humans to continue on earth, but living alongside other creatures, not destroying them.'

'I understand what you are saying,' says Xi.

'It's complete bullshit!' shouts Trumbushton, and winces, expecting his other hand to be paralysed, but Eleg does not react this time.

Xi continues: 'It is not possible, in human society, for a political leader to bring in policies that have such life-ending consequences for so many people. You ask too much of us, I fear.'

'Yet this is not a great deal more than many major countries did when the Covid-19 virus affected most of the world. That virus threatened 750,000 to 900,000 deaths. The ecological threat to the planet threatens much of mankind.

'As you know, recent human history has many examples of political leaders introducing policies that have led to the deaths of millions of humans, whether in Germany, China or Russia. And the USA was content to cause the death of over half a million people with two bombs in Japan in 1945,' says Johann.

'Not that bugbear again! For heaven's sake!' says President Trumbushton.

'And,' adds Olga, 'you have been carrying out policies for several decades, in the face of evidence provided by almost all the earth's leading scientists, that will have catastrophic consequences for the earth's ecology, and as such for your species, and countless other species. Billions of animals — and people — may die in a matter of years. Ants will not allow their species, or other creatures, to be destroyed in this way.'

'Ah ha!' exclaims Trumbushton, 'so it is ants! But no ants

can build a spaceship. Who is behind them?'

'You are ignorant,' says Johann. 'Ants have a planet which they have inhabited for millions of years. Their technology is far advanced on human technology. They organised the abduction of the 300,000 people who disappeared from earth 22 years ago.'

'What, the Phantom Mass Abduction! Come on, pull the other one,' says Trumbushton, 'it's got bells on!' and he winces again, but is spared further paralysis.

'Did you ever explain that mass disappearance?' asks Olga.

'That is beside the point. I won't believe ants did it,' says Trumbushton.

Xi intervenes: 'I am prepared to address the Chinese people,' he says. 'I cannot promise that changes will be made quickly, as you ask a great deal, but I can put forward to my central committee a set of revolutionary proposals to de-industrialise. I can also talk to other leaders, and ask them to cooperate, but of course I cannot make them follow suit.'

'It will need both of you. One is not enough,' explains Johann.

'Over my dead body,' says Trumbushton, who all too soon finds that the white sticky stuff has covered his left hand now, as a reaction to his obstinacy, so that both feet and both hands are now paralysed.

'We do not wish it to be over your dead body,' says Olga. 'We wish you and President Xi to agree to the demands and enable countless species to survive on earth. If it is over your dead body, then most of the human race will die as a consequence.'

'I need some evidence of the technological superiority of

the ant species. There is no evidence on earth of this.'

'You can see this spaceship, and you can see the robots they have created,' says Johann.

'There is no way on Earth that I believe that ants built this ship or the robots.'

'You are blind, Mr President,' says Johann, with emotion now affecting his voice. 'Humans have barely been in the universe five minutes compared to ants, which pre-date people by at least 130 million years. On another planet, they are the size of a Labrador dog, or a retriever.

'Their brains are half the size of a humans. Because a million ants can have a collective brain, their brainpower outweighs human brainpower thousands of times over. Their DNA is very different from the earth's ants. They have far greater cognitive ability. That is how they built spaceships like this.'

'You are running out of time,' adds Olga, as Trumbushton stares at Johann a bit nonplussed, for once. 'We will leave you for 12 hours Earth time, and then we will need a response.'

Trumbushton sleeps a while on the floor of the ship. When he wakes, President Xi makes further attempts to sway the US President.

'I am starting to see that there is some logic here,' says Xi. 'Our scientists do believe that it is possible that there are life forms more advanced than us, noting that the universe pre-dated human life by over 13 billion years, and pre-dated the earth by over 8.5 billion years.'

'Some creatures, maybe, with boggly eyes dangling at the end of a stick protruding from their head, or octopus-like slimy killers emerging in a grim and grisly way from a space hero's stomach. But not this!' suggests Trumbushton.

'You refer, I think, to films in the cinema, esteemed President,' counters X. 'I think it is beyond our knowledge how these creatures may be. Perhaps we are privileged enough to meet the ambassadors of a species not known before, albeit one not dissimilar to our ants.'

'They don't convince me. I think I may wake up from a bad dream and realise that this is all a prank played on me.'

'Please, esteemed President, this is very real,' pleads Xi. 'We know that very large numbers of people have died. We know that our opponents have killed political leaders and business leaders exactly as they have threatened. We know that, when they have warned that a million will die, very large numbers, estimated at 900,000 to 1.1 million, have died each time.'

'It also gives pause for thought,' he continues, 'that when we two were resisting the wish of other political leaders to agree the demands being made, it was the two of us who ended up in this spaceship.'

'But this so-called spaceship may just be an elaborate hoax, mocked up on some abandoned airfield, or cinema lot. Think of that! Maybe candid camera will suddenly turn up and say — "you have been had".'

'But it is also possible,' asserts Xi, 'that it is all true, and that human life on Earth is threatened, including all your people and all my people. Is that not something that concerns you? Do you want your legacy to be that you sacrificed all these billions of people out of your own selfishness and egotism?'

'As it happens,' concedes Trumbushton, 'I am concerned about some of my friends — billionaires, aspiring billionaires, multi-millionaires and their families, and the bimbos and internees I like to fuck. I won't necessarily lose sleep over others. I realise I should be concerned, but the fact of the matter is that it is me and my kind that matter in the end.'

'I am surprised,' responds Xi. 'I know our propagandists paint this picture of you. They point to the way the people of New Orleans were abandoned by a predecessor of yours in the last century when the city was flooded, because they were mainly poor. But I tended to think that there must be some goodness in you, that you could not be as bad as was being portrayed.'

'I think you might have to look very hard to find goodness,' laughs Trumbushton.

'You know I am a secret fan of your Bob Dylan?'

'That pinko no good wastrel!'

'A Nobel Prize winner, and a very fine poet. In his *Masters of War*, he sang:

Let me ask you one question
Is your money that good
Will it buy you forgiveness
Do you think that it could
I think you will find
When your death takes its toll
All the money you made
Will never buy back your soul.'

'Like I said, Communist claptrap. I don't need forgiveness. What's to forgive?'

'This is as much a Christian message as anything. Confucius, too, would agree with the essentials. Indeed, among the five virtues, Yi, Xin and Li are linked to this sentiment.'

'Confucius hocus pocus. It's all red to me. My Christianity says wealth is good, and I never did badly out of it.'

'Maybe the planet did badly, though.'

'Not where I live. It's just fine on my ranch.'

'I do not believe you have no good in you, President.'

'Of course, I try to be very good to myself, and to my wife, sometimes — but forget that. What matters is this rattlesnake-in-my-knapsack situation we have here. I'm convinced still that this is a trick, damn it, it's candid camera, for pity's sake…'

'What is this camera you refer to? You mentioned it before.'

'It is a television show, where a film camera is hidden, and people are tricked into doing stupid things or saying stupid things in front of the camera, which they have no knowledge of.'

'This is somewhat unlikely, I suggest. I do wish that you, Mr President, now reflect deeply on the clear and present danger the earth faces.'

'Heh, Jee, that is our phrase, you can't use that.'

'I have used it to try to press upon you the critical importance of this situation we are in.'

'Jee, I think you know and I know that we are going around in circles. I think there is only one way to deal with this. We must demand that we go to this other planet. If this is a spaceship, like they say, and they have come from there, then they can take us there. If I see their planet, I will believe them.'

'The world we know might be destroyed, the people all dead, before we get back.'

'Then we will stay on the other planet. This is the only way, Jee. I need to believe this species exists before I agree anything, and a visit to their planet is the only way.'

'Do you like your Laurel and Hardy?'

'Laurel and effing Hardy! Jeez, Jee, for a Commie bastard leader, you are a right jack in the box with all these surprises you spring on me.'

'You could be Oliver Hardy, and I could be Stan Laurel.'

'Are you calling me fat?'

'With respect, President Trumbushton, I would do no such thing.'

'Just get on with it.'

'You say: this is a nice mess you have gotten me into. And I say: here's another nice mess I have gotten you into.'

(laughing) 'You crack me up, Jee. You are one hell of a sonofabitch.'

'I don't understand, but I believe this may be a compliment.'

'Jee, will you come with me to this so-called planet?'

'I do not think you are giving me a choice.'

'Damn right. You have no choice.'

Trumbushton asks to speak to Olga, Johann and Eleg.

He states to them: 'As much as I appreciate the possible consequences, I strongly believe that the strength of US air, naval, sea and space forces would be too great for this Ant species and will defeat them. I do not consider that the human race is at risk.

'But I am a fair man, as is President Jee, and as a compromise, I will not order my forces to attack you. In return I wish to be taken with Jee to your planet.'

Olga and Johann look at each other, eyebrows raised,

Olga's having grown back by now. They look at Eleg, who says: 'Yes, it is agreed.'

Olga says to Presidents, Xi and Trumbushton: 'So be it. We will go. You will be put into a frozen state until we arrive. Cryogenics. You will be the same age when you arrive.'

'Cryo what...?' screams Trumbushton.

'It is cryogenics, like we on Earth have been developing, and you,' says Xi, 'freezing a person while they are alive. They seem to have taken it further than we have so far managed.'

'No way,' says Trumbushton.

'Of course, the people on Earth may die in the meantime,' says Eleg.

'Hell no...' starts Trumbushton, but Eleg immediately paralyses both him and Xi and takes them to the cryogenics room.

...

'Olga and Johann,' says Eleg, 'the two Presidents are now icicles. We have a job to do.'

'Which is?' asks Olga.

'I have had a word with the robots Cormor, Dorm, Fond and Pend and they will take this ship with the two Presidents to Howl. We must continue with an important task on the Blue Planet. Dorm and Fond are arranging for a small spaceship that is kept on a separate deck to be put into orbit for us to use when we have completed our task on the Blue Planet.'

'You mentioned the country Tanzania to Souad and Abdul,' says Olga.

'Yes, as the place for surviving humans,' adds Johann.

'That is correct,' says Eleg. 'I strongly suspect that the cousins have started stage two on the Blue Planet, now that stage one has not succeeded in prolonging Braiby life as it is known.'

'Stage two, I assume, is the mass murder that was warned about in the messages?' queries Johann.

'So Tanzania becomes the place for survivors after the mass of humans have died?' wonders Olga aloud.

'This is the plan,' says Eleg, 'but it is possible that very large numbers come to Tanzania. More than we allowed for. We need to go there to assess the situation on the ground. You will need to help me there.'

'You talk of us helping, but really you could manage on your own.'

'On the contrary, we are the Three Musketeers, one for all and all for one.'

'You are such a goof at times, Eleg. Where on Earth did you pick up that phrase?'

'Who knows? It is my software. Shall we go?'

And Eleg takes Johann and Olga to the polka dot-marked point near the lift ready for transport to the Blue Planet.

CHAPTER 8
Preparing for Species Changes on the Blue Planet

There is a change. The ants that live on the Blue Planet are taking over the plan to change the planet.

The robots from Howl are to be second string. Nothing is said. The ant world does not work like this. It is simply understood and acted upon.

In northern California, something highly unusual is happening at a number of large ant heaps in an ancient redwood forest, noted for its magnificent high trees.

The sister worker ants are busy harvesting bacterial spores in very large quantities.

The same is happening at ant heaps across the USA, across North, Central and South America and the Caribbean.

And much the same is happening in Europe, Africa, across the Asian continent and in Australasia. Even the Pacific islands.

The spores are dangerous, and need to be handled with care, as they produce a fatal toxin.

Ants take them to great fields of wheat and corn and grass fields and also to orchards in North America, Australia and Europe, and paddies of rice in Asia and millions more run amongst the wheat fields, maize fields and other crop pastures across Africa, excluding the Serengeti in Tanzania. They spread to fruit, cereal and vegetable crops and the pampas across Latin America and the Caribbean.

They deposit spores in the soil wherever they can, leaving it to develop and pass through the food chain, at least through any path where the requirement of zero oxygen is present. Others find their way to fruit orchards and fields of brassicas, tomatoes and other crops.

Tiny ants take the spores to airports and climb with them into the hand baggage of the pilots and of some stewards and stewardesses. Other ants climb into the air conditioning systems of office blocks, hospitals, schools, government buildings and apartment blocks wherever they can locate these.

The spores are also put into the water supply in every community, from wells to reservoirs.

In addition, ants climb into cars at petrol stations, at traffic lights, in car parks and in traffic jams, while also placing the spores on car tyres, to ensure they are carried far and wide.

No village, town or city is spared, wherever there is human life.

Other ants, in great numbers:

— head to food wrapping plants, where fresh food is wrapped in plastic, or cardboard, or both, and spread the spores wherever they see food exposed. Many ants are killed in the process, but enough find their way past the extreme hygiene conditions to inflict deadly damage;

— find their way into canning plants, and manage to drop spores into the contents of cans of meat stew, kidney beans, baked beans, lamb curry, anchovies, tuna etc.;

— pass to wasps and bees to assist in wider dissemination in towns and cities;

— pass to flocks of swallows, swifts, arctic terns, wheatears, swans, geese, storks and falcons, all of which specialise in covering long distances across continents.

Thousands of millions of ants are involved in the spreading of the spores. Many succumb in the process, but they travel in groups and in most cases enough survive to deliver the spores.

The spores produce clostridium botulinum, the H group, exposure of a two billionth of a gram of which is enough to kill a person, initially through paralysis. Vital organs will then fail, over any time between half a day and three days.

Two grams can kill a billion people, but in practice much more is needed because of the global spread of the population.

. . .

Meanwhile, an international symposium is taking place on security against the new threat.

Ants have been identified as a dangerous spreader of poison and a threat in themselves. Initially, this threat was seen as coming from hemlock, but countless reports of botulism from many parts of the world are ushering in a change of focus.

Some conspiracy theorists' postulate that ants have planned all the deaths to date, but most decision-makers and strategists discount this argument as beyond the realms of possibility. The symposium ends when, one by one, a number of delegates die for no known reason, but with a suspicion of botulism.

The governments of each of the major northern hemisphere countries, and of many smaller countries, have been placed on high alert.

Guards have been placed outside the homes of politicians, well-known celebrities and numerous high-level business people; and also, at military posts, at reservoirs, at important tourist sites, and on international borders.

There is an edict in every country emphasising the need to stay at home, and not to drink tap water unless vigorously boiled. Millions are torn between leaving their homes for bottled water or staying at home and risking their tap water.

With growing anxiety about tap water, and about leaving home to buy safe water, as the death toll mounts rapidly, there is a new craze of drinking urine.

Online 'Living with the Ant Threat' sites explain how one may purify urine by passing through different containers holding sand, stones, vegetation etc., one container at a time. But they also stress the benefit of drinking urine unpurified, the first few times it is passed through.

Urine, say the sites, contains nitrogen, potassium, calcium and sodium, which are all good for survival.

After 2–3 times re-used, urine becomes too concentrated to be drunk easily.

The message is: drinking urine is your best hope of survival, but survival doesn't last long.

Social media is abuzz:

— *Now they are really taking the piss.*

— *They are taking our piss.*

— *They will have us eating shit next.*

— *I will die before I drink my own piss.*

— *My cat drinks its own piss and doesn't seem to mind.*

— *But we are not animals.*

— *But if we can't go out and can't drink tap water, what do we do?*

— *My mum said, 'sod it' and drank tap water and she is now dead (a hundred thousand likes).*

— *All my family is dead apart from me, froze like statues, couldn't breathe, couldn't breathe at all, died (two million likes).*

— *I think I will drink my piss if I can last a bit longer.*

— *Is your piss sweeter if you only drink coke?*

— *Is it hell?*

— *Does your piss make you high if you get high on cocaine?*

— *May do.*

— *Not likely.*

— *Have you been outside? It's like the apocalypse on the streets.*

— *I think we are all going to die.*

— *I am sick of this whole thing. I would kill myself if I was not going to die anyway.*

— *The information we get is too confusing. What the hell are we supposed to do?*

— *Kill all the damn ants.*

Few people leave their homes, and those who do venture out in public appear furtive and wary. Dead bodies lie on pavements wherever one looks. Many cars are parked at odd angles, with the occupants dead inside.

Social media is ferociously busy with theories about the missing US President Trumbushton and President Xi:

— *Big fat bastards ran away, didn't they, couldn't face the music.*

— *Maybe they are negotiating.*

— *Yea, but who with? We never get told nothing!*

— *Think they have run off together. Two of a kind.*

— But they are polar opposites. Arch capitalist and arch communist.

— Opposites attract.

— I think Trumbushton wouldn't be seen dead with Xi Jin Ping.

— Maybe he's playing Xi Jin ping pong with Xi Jin Ping?

— Not funny.

— I don't like this silence. We've heard nothing in ages.

— You'd think their number 2s would say something.

— Maybe they were having number 2s and fell down the loo.

— Word is that they don't know; nobody knows.

— Like media blackout?

— Yea, probs top secret negotiations with the bastard mass killers. All hush, hush.

— Hope they can do something. We are all dying here.

— Dying by the bucketload here. Can't drink, nowt to eat, can't go out. Can't sleep for worry. It's crap.

— My family is dead, my cat is dead, and my budgie, my neighbours are dead, my friends are dead.

— Tell us something new

Much of the social media babble surrounds the ants' messages, where they were specifically placed, and what they were written with:

— How did the ants get there to kill these people? Who took them?

— Why do ants hate us?

— They say it is our turn. Too many species have died.

— Ants can't write words that humans can read. Someone is behind it.

— *The messages are clever and planned. Must be a big brain.*

— *We have taken it all too far. Perhaps we will learn about killing off other species if we also suffer.*

— *But we are the clever species, we are needed. They can't kill off our species. Who will save the planet?*

— *Maybe that is the point. Maybe the planet will only be saved if we go.*

— *Maybe we had a chance to save the planet, and we blew it.*

— *Think that eco-terrorists run all this. They hide behind ants so they don't get blamed for the deaths.*

— *There is no social media trail that can be found; no online messages that can be traced suggesting eco activists are involved. None at all.*

— *I can't believe ants found the Nile bed stones and took them to the Sphinx; ants are not that strong.*

— *And that coral in Australia, what gave them that idea?*

— *It's too clever by half, done by little critters that couldn't rub two brain cells together. Don't fit.*

— *Ants are amazing. Their colonies are like big cities, and work like clockwork. Maybe there's more to an ant than meets the eye.*

— *I got an ant in my eye once. That ant met my eye.*

— *Stop gabbling.*

— *They are programmed to do things in a group. They can't think for themselves.*

— *So what? We can think for ourselves, and what good has that done us?*

— *Are we done for?*

— *Must be somewhere we can escape to, top of Mont Blanc I fancy.*

— *Or Himalayas. Bit cold for ants up there.*

— *So how long do you live up there, unless you become a Sherpa?*

— *Can't get there. Transport is seizing up left right and centre.*

— *The Four Horses of the Apocalypse will arrive.*

— *Don't start all that Bible stuff, that's all we need.*

— *It's all predicted in the Bible. We've all become too immoral.*

— *I just don't think that helps, when we are up the proverbial shit creek without a paddle.*

— *It is like we are in a village engulfed by a mighty avalanche, except this time the world is the village.*

— *It's all too weird.*

...

Over the next 24 hours, social media report more and more mass fatalities.

In the vast Revolution Square in Tehran, Iran, where a million women enrobed in chadors celebrated in 1980 the anniversary of the anti-Shah revolution, and where a third of a million are expected for the anniversary today, only three women arrive in the morning. There are no taxis, no buses, no passenger cars, no bicycles. The three women who have arrived had been on a four day fast and had been in their homes, so had not encountered the botulism bacterium. Corpses litter the streets, in a variety of odd angles; cars are parked in odd places, with drivers and family members dead inside.

The three women begin to realise the enormity of what is taking place. Soon they too become paralysed and they die the next day from the plague.

At the Camp Nou stadium in Barcelona, two fans Paco and Charo approach the stadium. The posters outside advertise today's El Clásico match with Real Madrid. The stadium, normally full for such a match, stands empty. There is no security, nobody opening the gates, no TV, no radio, and above all no fans.

Paco and Charo hang around for an hour. They think of the bodies they passed on the way, the numerous crashed cars, the dead cyclists. They begin to put two and two together as to why 80,000 fans are missing. Paco and Charo hang their heads and depart for home.

Once home, they soon become paralysed and die the next day.

In Mecca, four Moslems arrive at Masjid-al-Haram, when two or two and a half million people are expected that day, as is not uncommon. These four have been fasting for six days, cut off from all media.

The four Moslems die within 24 hours.

In Tien Mien Square, near the cordoned off Forbidden City in Beijing, China, a major national parade, expected to attract a few hundred thousand people, attracts just five. These five, stand around for nearly two hours, talking about all the corpses they have seen on the streets, the car drivers, dead at their wheels, the buses full of dead people, including a driver dead at the wheel. One or two report social media stories of piles of corpses in other Chinese cities; one says there are photos of the Yangtze river full of corpses, to the point where it is forming a dam at one particular bend in the river.

Slowly it dawns on them that they are witness to a tragedy of very great proportions, even by Chinese standards, and then drift away.

Outside Buckingham Palace in London, there is not the usual large crowd of tourists for the Changing of the Guard. One man, his cane, and his dog arrive. They notice the flag at half mast, and the man lowers his head and taps his cane on the ground. The dog lowers his nose.

There is no guard, and no changing of the guard. The dog nuzzles his master's leg, suggesting it is not worth staying. The man agrees.

While there is still a functioning social media, reports come of:

— pile ups on motorways, and blockages in most town and city centres, as drivers become paralysed or (in many cases) die at the wheel;

— crashes of aeroplanes all over the world, with numerous panic-stricken messages coming from pilots or their co-pilot reporting paralysis, weakness and an inability to continue flying;

— governments in every country ceasing to function, including local government;

— emergency services finding it difficult to get to most of the car and aeroplane crashes as the traffic is blocked everywhere as a consequence of drivers dying at the wheel. In little time, the emergency services themselves are unable to function due to most personnel themselves having died;

— people who only drink bottled water and don't drive finding most of their neighbours and their relatives dead;

— prisoners in gaols around the world noticing the warders have died, and in many cases escaping (only to die themselves); a number of prisoners, neglect to leave, having heard rumours of mass deaths, but die nonetheless from the water in the prisons;

— the pavements of many towns and cities now full of dead bodies, with just the odd person walking gingerly past all the blocked cars and endless corpses...

But in little time the bottled water drinkers who don't drive also succumb to the plague. There is no bottled left for them. Most processed food is now affected.

Social media is soon quieter than it has been since its very earliest days.

Many of the messages report paralysis taking over and warn not to drink tap water. Poignantly, many messages end halfway through:

'Am paralysed, can't...'

'Don't know what wrong, fuck...'

'My fingers can hardly...I'm udimg mi toas... i'm niw usung mi noas'

'All my family are...'

'My sister is paralysed, my brother is dead, I am starting to feel...'

In a household of five in Berwick-upon-Tweed, one has died that morning, mouth and arms paralysed, and heart stopped. One died at work, after drinking coffee from the coffee machine, and becoming paralysed, and one died in the car on the way home; a fourth died in the evening after having a drink of orange squash.

The last one, Ned, walks out to look out across the estuary of the Tweed to the mournfully grey sea, above which cowers a contemplative dark grey sky. There are very few people out and about, even for Berwick. There is a woman with her two dogs. She and Ned exchange a nod. With darkness now falling, no lights are coming on in the old town within the ancient city's walls, or across the bay at Spittle, whose lights normally twinkle in the evening.

It is as though the world is slowly coming to an end. The woman with her two dogs, collapses, and the dogs try to wake her, then decide soon to curl up around her head.

Ned sits on a bench, notes the full moon with its mysterious face. He thinks of Olga — bright, brilliant, ecologically obsessed Olga, with her mercurial love of Bach's cello suite and Captain Beefheart's Trout Mask Replica. Her Indian dad and German-Danish mother, and her slight figure, sharp mind and quirkiness. He recalls their last words together 20 odd years ago — 'See you on Sunday, my angel', 'Can't wait' — their last kiss, before she disappeared.

What did happen to Olga? He would never know.

He notes his hands, legs and feet are now paralysed, and he lies down on the bench and shuts his eyes for the last time.

....

A woman squats by her son. Below them is a calm, exquisite lake and around them mountain peaks, blue-grey cones as though recent volcanos, with a thin coating of snow at the top. The peaks circle the lake, which goes by the name of Atitlan.

The woman and her son wear traditional Guatemalan peasant clothes. They are in the shadow of a simple hut.

The woman says: There is a legend, told by our elders, and to them by their elders, and so on back to the beginning of life.

There was a time when the great whale of the ocean departed the waves for land. The great whale was as enormous as a mountain and had a mouth as wide as a valley.

The whale started swallowing the people. The more they ran, the more it swallowed. It swallowed and swallowed and swallowed, until all the people were eaten up.

The whale was too heavy to find its way back to sea. It lay there and moaned. It had a stomach-ache so painful that it could not breathe. It let out an ear-splitting cry. The mountains shook at the sound of this mighty cry.

Then the whale started to be sick. It was sick for seven days and seven nights. And as it sicked up the contents of its stomach, it writhed with the pain, so that the sick spread all over the mountains and the valley.

And eventually the whale stopped being sick and curled up and died.

And on the mountains grew new flowers, new bushes, new trees. And in the valley, new creatures emerged, from new breeds of hedgehog and mouse, to new breeds of hog and puma. And the new creatures fed off the new plants and, if they were carnivores, the new creatures.

And the dead whale sank into the valley and became its new lakebed, which soon filled with water. Fish, amphibians and water lilies followed. The creatures drank from the water to quench their thirst.

There was harmony in the new world.

The son looks at his mother and asks: is the whale going to come back again?

The mother answers: dear Emilio, I think this was just a legend. There was no whale. But I think we are now at last seeing the whale, swallowing up all the people of the world. It certainly feels that way. Perhaps it will lead to a harmony in the world that has long been absent.

...

Twitter closes down. There is no final farewell tweet.

On Facebook, there is a report that all the employees at Twitter headquarters are dead.

But soon, there is a report from Facebook in Kingston, Jamaica that all the employees at Facebook offices in America have tragically died or are incapacitated. Soon after, no part of Facebook functions, not even in Greenland.

Instagram posts *in memoriam* vlogs for the Kardashian family, now 48 strong with many children, and even two-year-old grandchildren with their Nappylogs; there are also *in memoriam* vlogs for the highly successful Rumpelstiltskin site, and the Little Red Riding Hood site, and their many offshoots, as well as many thousands of other Instagram accounts.

The BBC then reports that Instagram has closed down.

The BBC website closes down, and most European and US news organisations follow suit. The same occurs in China, India, across much of Asia, Africa, Latin America and in Australia and New Zealand.

For those people that are still online, there is now very little online to access. There is a site in Nuuk, the capital of Greenland, another in Norilsk, in northern Siberia, a satellite-linked site at Villa las Estrellas in the Chilean part of

Antarctica, and there are sites in Tanzania, including in Dar es Salaam, calling for natives of the Serengeti to come home. Almost no other sites are operational.

A message in Inuit and English on the Nuuk site reads:

The world as we knew it is entering a very long sleep, with just the occasional wink.

Chapter 9
All Roads Lead to Tanzania

1. In Lesotho

Middle aged, her deeply wrinkled skin, folding over sad eyes, reflects a tortured life. Her hands arthritic, she loosely holds the hands of an old man who has just arrived in her tiny remote village in the mountain kingdom of Lesotho, southern Africa.

'I remember him like it was yesterday,' she says, 'his tiny fingers holding my pinkie, his smile that could make you melt.

'His oldest brother had developed leprosy, and had to go to the Botshabelo leper settlement, seven km from Maseru. He sadly died there.

'Three sisters and his other brother had developed Aids. My three sisters developed Aids, my brother too. I was HIV positive for years. Aids was taking so many of us in those days, and they had no chance.

'Remember our tiny village, a hamlet really, just a short distance from Malealea Lodge in Lesotho, near that Welcome to Gates of Paradise sign. Paradise for some perhaps; hell for those with Aids.

'I recall our neighbours lived in a stylish Basotho Hat building — a round hut with an upwardly pointing thatched roof, which Europeans would give their eye teeth for.

'You and I came together for a simple life of Khotso, Pula, Nala — peace, rain and plenty. Luck did not follow us there. So much tragedy in a place of such beauty.

'The Swedish couple were childless, and they promised to give our new baby Tuma a good life, just outside their capital, Stockholm. So we gave Tuma up.'

Motlatsi held Mathabo's wrists and pressed a little more firmly. He avoided her hands because of the arthritic pain.

'It was the hardest thing to do, to give up one's child,' says Mathabo.

'Did you keep a photo of him?'

'I kept one the Swedish couple sent me. I think it's in that little hole up there,' and she points to a shaded spot just below the thatch, where a cobweb covers a hole. He pulls out a slightly creased, yellowed photograph and squints hard to see the child's face better.

'Such a handsome boy,' he says, 'with your eyes,' and passes her the photo.

'Ah, but not that you can see my eyes anymore,' she replies, as she casts her eyes down.

'Love has perfect recall,' he replies.

She puckers her lips and kisses the baby's face, then turns the photo over.

'This must be Tuma's Swedish name,' she says, pointing. 'Joh... something.'

And she passes it back to him.

'Johann. Yes, I am sure. Johann,' he says.

'I wonder where Johann is now,' wondered Mathabo aloud.

. . . .

203

2. Border of Tanzania with Burundi

There is chaos on the northern frontier of Tanzania, at the border crossing of Mabamba Gisuru, where tens of thousands are camped on the Burundi side trying to cross through.

In the last days of social media, word got out that people in the Serengeti area would be allowed to live. This went viral, and the few survivors from the ant-spread botulism plague trekked over vast distances to try to reach there.

One middle-aged man, closely cropped hair, unshaven, skin more chestnut than chocolate, is screaming at the border guards:

'I've lost all my family. I've travelled 8,000 miles in the most trying circumstances, I've family here. I left here with my parents when I was three. I beg you. Let me in, please!'

A woman shouts: 'The plague has killed my sisters, my brothers, parents, cousins, in laws, even my children. I am the only one left. I go back four generations, when my family left Dar Es Salaam. Please give me a chance.'

Behind her, Souad, Abdul and Mohammed, very bedraggled in appearance, look on, wondering what case they can make to gain entry.

Animals come unusually near to the throng of people, including zebra and giraffe. People have in recent weeks learnt to their cost that any human with a weapon is set upon quickly by flying ants that poison them until they put down their weapons.

Bit by bit, some larger animals realise humans are not able to kill with guns anymore. It is now an even contest of speed, strength and guile.

In addition, vehicles have been immobilised, in part by ecologists who support the ant cause, and call themselves Ants Ally (generally known as Aunt Sally).

Insect allies of the ants have also helped immobilise hundreds of millions of petrol or diesel-fuelled vehicles across the world by filling the petrol or diesel tanks with their bodies and clogging them all up.

Electric vehicles have not escaped. Powerful ants attack their brake cables and transmission cables with their mandibles, and tiny insects have found a way into their batteries and caused them to leak to the point where they no longer have a function

As such, with precious few vehicles still working, there are crowds of people in a blind panic to reach the land where they believe they can survive, but only have their power of persuasion — plus the weight of numbers — to try to enter.

Only a tiny proportion of the world's population has survived the mass botulism poisoning, but perhaps 350–400,000 — out of the 7.5 billion there were before the botulism and related attacks — have managed to survive and have found their way to different border posts around Tanzania. Perhaps twice this number remains inside Tanzania.

Those outside the country are not necessarily aware that ants await them inside Tanzania, as it is only in one part of Tanzania, in the Serengeti region in the northern part of the country, where ants will not kill Braibies.

A woman speaks out to the crowd around Souad, Abdul and Mohammed. 'We won't all get into Tanzania. We need a way of deciding. Those who can go in will have a good chance of surviving; those outside will have a very slim chance; they will be in the hands of fate.'

'What do you suggest, Alina?' asks a man nearby.

'The only fair system is a system of random chance, drawing lots.'

'What about Tanzanians? We should have a prior right,' shouts a woman.

'This is a new situation,' replies Alina. 'There is no prior right to anything. I have spoken to a guard, who says one in a hundred may come through. I suggest that I arrange a system to see who gets to go, and who needs to stay. Put your hands up if you agree.'

Almost everyone in the vicinity puts their hand up.

'I will come up with a lottery system by tomorrow,' says Alina.

There are camps all over countries neighbouring Tanzania, including Rwanda, Burundi, Mozambique, Kenya, Uganda, D R Congo, Zambia, Malawi, and even Zimbabwe.

In the Burundi and Uganda camps, in a patch of ground where the earth is generally less stony, attempts are made to dig a tunnel into Tanzania. The guards in the camps have little interest in preventing escape, for the most part, so little attention is paid to the digging on their part.

In one case, in a camp in Burundi, the tunnel goes on for over 200 metres, but collapses as soon as people start trying it out.

In a camp in Uganda, there are two old men from Vietnam who have experience of the Chu Chi tunnels in the Vietnam War. They explain what is needed, how to make the tunnel secure, how to ensure that it is going in the right direction and so on.

The tunnel penetrates under the Tanzanian border and about 120 refugees find a way through before the guards notice the long queue to enter the tunnel and put a stop to it.

People are dying every day in the camps, so low are supplies of drinkable water, and so limited are food supplies. No charities operate any longer, as the management personnel of the charities have succumbed to the plague, as have the great majority of the charity workers.

...

Johann, Eleg and Olga

Olga, Johann and Eleg arrive in an arid landscape, the setting sun casting a red glow across the jagged sandstone terrain. Trees are scarce, standing solitary amidst a sea of rocks. A few vultures circle high above and insects scurry everywhere, near their feet, but there is little evident mammal life.

On one lonely but well-endowed tree, a weaver bird has somehow managed to weave one of its magnificent nests, and it stands out majestically in the evening's red glow. Whether this bird has a mate, or can find one in this unfriendly terrain, who knows?

'What reports are you getting on the rescue of the Blue Planet?' asks Olga, as she polishes off her daily portion of honey.

'On the bigger picture, success is reported on many fronts,' says Eleg. 'The Blue Planet continents Asia, Europe, Australasia and the Americas, are mostly free of Braibies, with limited exceptions. There are small pockets of Braibies left, in Greenland, in the Yukon in Canada, in northern Siberia and in

Australia, where a number of Aborigines in the outback have survived. These people are expected to live from the land and the sea, so will not be a threat to other species.'

'That's something then, if Native Americans, Inuit, Aborigine and Siberian hunters and gatherers survive.'

'Much of Africa is also free of Braibies, I am told, but we did not foresee how things may develop in Tanzania.'

'What is happening in Tanzania?'

'Quite large numbers have arrived there, and a large number of Tanzanians are still alive, as the ants and their allies were more sparing there.'

'What numbers do you think remain?' asks Johann.

'My masters had wanted at most 500,000 Braibies left in the Serengeti area,' responds Eleg. 'The reports suggest that over a million are there, or on the borders, but not much more than this.'

'That's still an extraordinary change!' exclaims Olga, eyebrows raised.

'About 7.5 billion dead — based on the figures when we left the Blue Planet,' adds Johann.

'We have to decide how many of those Braibies left are to die,' says Eleg, 'it is not yet clear how any decisions are to be made by those on the ground.'

'Am I right in thinking that you are hinting that we have to gather some evidence, to help with this decision?' asks Olga.

'You mean in Tanzania?' asks Johann.

'Yes. We are close to the new Braiby home. I will need both of you,' says Eleg. 'I need you to help communicate with Braibies, while I communicate with the ants.'

'Wow,' says Olga, 'I've always wanted to go to Tanzania.'

'It may be close to my homeland,' says Johann.

'Your homeland?'

'My parents told me that I was born in southern Africa.'

'Wow.'

'Be ready for some hard work,' said Eleg.

There is a distant sound of drumming, which spreads around the horizon.

Smoke beyond a distant copse of trees suggests Braibies. Ants confirm the same to Eleg. They head that way, with Johann ahead, and Eleg gently holding Olga's hand with a middle leg, as he walks with the other five legs.

As they near the smoke, they get a sense of the size of the crowd there, which stretches off into the distance. They stop briefly at a stream, where Olga and Johann take a drink. The smoke arises from an impala being cooked, and dozens of people are hoping to get a portion.

'Is anyone in charge here?' asks Olga.

A woman answers in Swahili.

Eleg says to Olga and Johann, 'She is concerned about me. Doesn't like me being here. She also says that we need to go to the village to the north of here, inside Tanzania, where there are some English speakers who know more.'

Johann thanks the woman, and they head north, Olga accepting an offer of a piece of sweetcorn as they depart. She eats it readily, having had nothing familiar except honey for a long time, and she offers Johann a bite, which he accepts readily.

Eleg approaches an ant heap en route, a little way from the main path. Ants confirm to him that there is another human village further north. He tells them about the phrase Braibies, but it doesn't translate.

They also confirm that there are now far fewer humans about, but many more are now in the countryside, living by eating animals.

...

'Who are you?' asks the English speaker, as they enter the village.

'I'm Olga, and this man is Johann, while this is a robot called Eleg, who is a part genius, part idiot,' replies Olga. 'We represent the ants who are behind this change to the world.'

'If I hadn't seen what I have seen in recent weeks, I would think you had walked off the pages of a science fiction book. For some weird reason, though, I believe you.'

'Who are you?'

'I'm Habiba.'

'Hi, Habiba, is there anyone here who knows what is happening with the return of mankind to Serengeti?'

'It's complete chaos. People have come from far and wide, from Europe, Asia and all over Africa. Even local people are being pushed out.'

'Is anyone in charge?'

'The government has collapsed, as most of its members died, as did the opposition and most of the civil servants. Few police or army are still alive. There are no internet communications. There is drumming to guide people where to go. A few self-appointed people are trying to make sense of things.'

'Are the main buildings still there?' asks Olga.

'Just a few, otherwise there is a lot of rubble there. Insects have begun to eat away at the foundations of many of the buildings — ants and termites mainly, I'm told. Only the library and main administrative buildings are still intact. There is also little left of tarmac roads, as vegetation begins to extend its roots in intricate ways in and out of the surface. No cars or other vehicles are working. They are fast become rust buckets.'

'You seem well informed.'

'More than your idiot-genius robot. Doesn't say a lot, does he?'

'Only when it needs to,' replies Olga.

'I was an administrator in Rwanda, just over the border. I came here as soon as the messages came through about the return to Serengeti. I try to keep my ear close to the ground.'

'What is the situation in Rwanda?'

'From what I could see, the great majority of people died from the plague. There are corpses everywhere, and there is nobody to take them away. Stinks to high heaven in the tropical heat. It's so intense, you nearly suffocate. Perhaps a few tens of thousands made it to the borders with Tanzania. Probably even more since I was given that information. I imagine quite a lot of them are still there.'

'That is very helpful. Are you coping OK?'

'Ha. Most of the known world is dead and she asks am I coping! You know, I had an aunt in Rwanda when the massacres of her people the Tutsis occurred. 70% of them wiped out in 12 weeks or so. She talked of how part of her mind stopped living then and flew to a place over the mountains to curl into a ball and shrivel up. But part of her mind knew only to survive. This part began, she said, as a small seed, but grew into a strong flower. Others experienced the same. We need this seed in us, and we need the seed to grow to strong vibrant flowers. Then we can begin things afresh.'

'That is a positive and powerful image,' says Olga.

'I hope so. It was for us.'

'Is there anyone we can meet who is trying to organise the people here?'

'There is an indigenous woman Moreen in a village about 20 miles directly to the east of here. There is only one functioning road, just follow that. Moreen is a serious organiser.'

Eleg says to her in Swahili: 'In the new world, you will be an important player.'

Habiba smiles.

'Not such an idiot then,' she says in Swahili, and she holds up a hand to wave as they set off.

'What did you say to her?' asks Olga.

'That's for me to know and you to find out,' says Eleg.

'You're just a charmer, pure charmer, I reckon.'

There is a distant sound of drumming.

…… ……

They follow Habiba's directions and reach the village as the bright red sun begins to disappear below the horizon. They are directed to a house near the centre for Moreen. The moonlight is just bright enough for them to find her.

A woman with white hair and features that reflect elements of both south India and east Africa is perched on a stool on the veranda.

'Are you Moreen?' asks Olga.

'I am. Are you from the aliens who are behind all this?'

'Sort of,' says Olga. 'Have you worked out that it is aliens who are behind it?'

'Well, I just read all the messages that came out on social media, when we still had it. I just put two and two together. Unlike most people, I believed there was a spaceship, and probably aliens. I guess I also believed deep down that we as a human race had been so disastrously reckless in our treatment of our planet for so long that perhaps it needed someone from the outside to teach us a few lessons.'

'You and me are two of a kind,' says Olga.

'It doesn't make it any easier, all this tragedy, mind you,' says Moreen, 'I have seen black rhinos nearly die out as a species; I've felt for every rhino that passed away, my emotions bound up with the imagined emotions of those rhinos.

'It has been similar with Verreaux's sifakas lemurs, beautiful but rare creatures, with white fur ringing a cheeky small black face. I have screamed at officials, written protest letters, and even visited poachers and drunk evil liquor with them in a vain attempt to stop them killing threatened species. I've been through it, too, with species of tree frog and butterfly.

'But this mass extermination has really taken me aback. I did see the ants' message on social media, and I got the point that it is humans' turn to face near extinction. But to see so many loved ones die, and such a huge death toll. It has been hard, very hard.'

'Sure,' says Olga. 'Our hearts are not designed well for tragedy, even if many of us have from our early years imbued the Buddhist philosophy of treating all creatures as equal, including ourselves.'

'My masters had to act,' interjects Eleg, 'because their own species and so many other species on the Blue Planet that are essential for ecological balance were threatened by human activity.'

'Am I right to assume from your shape that your masters are ants?'

'Yes.'

'They are massive, the size of a Labrador dog or a retriever,' says Johann, 'they have their own planet light years away.'

'Have you been there?'

'Well, I know it's hard to believe,' says Olga, 'but they freeze you in the spaceship. It's called cryogenics.'

'Like cry me a river?'

'Ha, if only it were. Anyhow, you are frozen solid. Then you wake up years later on this other planet with two moons and a green sky.'

'It's not hard to believe, Olga, it's completely unbelievable. It's like pure science fiction. But, you know, I'm just glad to meet you both, in the context of all that is happening. And I won't question the truth of what you say.'

'So, can you tell us a bit about what is happening on the ground?' asks Olga. 'Take the borders, are there a lot of problems on the borders, with people trying to get in?'

'There has been a host of problems. With so much of the population dying, even here in Tanzania law and order has broken down for the most part. There are no charity workers left by the border, of course. All left, and probably most died when they did so, I guess. There are border guards who seek to protect the border at key border points, but they are overwhelmed by the huge numbers of people trying to come in.'

'How do things stand now? Do you get a sense of how many people are outside Tanzania trying to get in?'

'It is hard. There's no media anymore, so you don't get good information from around the country. I see travellers come through that give me an idea of what's going on. Most talk of large numbers on the borders, chaos, and a threat of starvation, and widespread disease.'

'Are people in Tanzania managing to get food and drink?' asks Johann.

'It's strange in a way. With the populations in Tanzania dropping by many millions almost overnight, the supermarkets are full of food, but there is no refrigeration. So, there is plenty of canned food, but little fresh food. Everything fresh goes off quickly in a hot climate, as you may imagine.'

'What about fruit and vegetable growing areas?'

'People have raided these for food, but it does not last. Everybody will have to go back to living off the land — which some still do, of course, but not enough of us. For the present, animals are being killed for food, but with knives and spears now, rather than guns.'

'Are the rivers clean?'

'Well, with microplastics everywhere, they are not as clean as they may be, but the water is probably drinkable. I understand that they are now botulism free. There is also no shortage of canned and bottled drinks, for now.'

'I need to ask,' says Eleg, 'whether the population needs to be culled further.'

'Culled? We are not seals!' exclaims Moreen.

215

'This is a simple decision, for us, but a hard one for you,' says Eleg, trying to explain. 'The ants had in mind leaving about 500,000 people, to start off the human story again, but this time to kickstart the new story in a way that would mean living with the planet, and not destroying it.

'If we assume there are now around one million people, or slightly more, could this work, with the eco balance here? Or do we need to reduce it to achieve a balance?'

'You are asking me to guide you in making a decision on whether half a million should live or not. I'm not going there, thank you very much, just not going there. I'm a simple Indo-African from Tanzania, not anything special like a guru.'

'Moreen, Eleg does not have morals, as a robot,' says Olga, but in his clumsy way he is trying to give you the chance of sparing the lives of half a million people. If they can make a new life here, and help maintain an ecological balance here, then they could perhaps be allowed to live.'

'That is a little easier, I guess,' responds Moreen.. 'But why can't people just spread out into Uganda, Kenya, Burundi, Zambia and the other surrounding countries?'

'The world is so damaged,' says Olga. 'Much has to happen in these countries to allow the ecological balance to be restored, and this will take time, at least one generation, possibly two.'

'I see,' says Moreen, 'so it is a question of Tanzania maintaining a population of around a million, as the people adapt to a life of farming, husbandry, fishing, traditional crafts, small trades, horticulture, and living simply?'

'Essentially, that is it?' replies Olga, 'Would you agree, Eleg?'

'I think that this is the decision to be taken, yes.'

'Well, I don't have a lot to go on as yet, 'says Moreen, 'Historically, this was a pastoral country, I know that much, and I would think that, with a country of this size, a million could live here. It is far, far smaller than the 57 to 58 million I think were living here before the plague. On balance, I think it should be given a try.'

'I will tell my masters,' says Eleg. 'The objective for them is that the Braibies are no longer a society of dog eat dog, Man eat dog, Man eat Planet. I can report that this has been accomplished.'

'I think that means it is agreed,' says Olga.

'No more Man eat Planet sounds especially good,' says Johann, smiling.

'Damn right, can we open the borders?' asks Moreen. 'That would be brilliant, as it would make things much easier, and so much less tense and fraught all round our borders.'

'The people outside can come in,' says Eleg, 'but then, when they are in, the borders need to be closed again. After a few days, in any event. We want to let the ecosphere in other parts of the world recover. In Tanzania, the whole country, the plague will end, but not elsewhere.'

'I understand,' says Moreen. 'That's all good news, in the circumstances. I will ask the drummers to send an initial message now. In the morning, I will get some messages out to the guards near here and ask them to send out riders to the other border posts with the same message.'

Moreen explains the message in Swahili to a young woman, Minna, who is waiting next to her. Minna runs off to the nearest drummers.

. . . .

Olga and Moreen

'Sometimes it seems civilisation is back to front,' says Moreen, thinking aloud.

'How do you mean?' asks Olga.

'The world in which native peoples lived for thousands of years with nature was so harmonious. Species developed and multiplied. The ecosphere was stabilised. Even after tens of thousands of years. Now, we live against the interests of the ecosphere in the way we live. And hundreds of thousands of species suffer the consequences.'

'Population growth put some pressure on people to change, I guess.'

'But other species manage this successfully. They don't destroy the planet when they multiply excessively. They have times when large numbers die, whether through disease or starvation. The world also goes through big changes of temperature over tens of millennia, which can help to balance things. We used to keep control of population through wars and disease, I guess.'

'But we can control so many diseases now, and we even have a cure for many cancers. I deeply dislike a very great deal of what has happened to the human race, but the progress on people's health is surely a good thing.'

'But did we find a cure for cancer only to cause an incurable cancer-like disease suffered by the planet that was our home, I wonder? A paradox. Smallpox gone but Planet Earth succumbs to humanpox.'

'Ha, clever.'

'Oh, just a badly thought-out comment. Nothing really'.

'It is an extraordinary irony of modern humans. We know so much but we apply that knowledge like we have learnt nothing. I sometimes wonder about Socrates, Buddha and Confucius.'

'You are having me on. You wonder about great minds from ancient times! Some people wonder about why their nails grow so quickly, or why their hair is greasy. But no, that is far too simple.'

'They were contemporaneous. Millennia later, Buddhists, as a whole, have not been acquisitive people. For all their large numbers, they have mostly been able to live in harmony with the planet. Those following Confucius the same. With a family-oriented culture, and deep tradition that all follow, the Chinese have been able to live in harmony with the earth, even while having the largest population of any nation. Like Buddhists, they until recent times have not been acquisitive like those in western countries. But Socrates is different.'

'So what wrongs has Socrates committed?'

'Socratic thought is the basis of European intellectual tradition since the Greek and Roman empires ruled in one part of the world. There was then a 1,400-year gap, I guess, when civilisation moved eastwards a bit, but when modern Europe was kickstarted by the industrial revolution and modern slavery, Socratic thinking provided its intellectual underpinning.

'I think that Confucius and Buddha provided a fairly complete moral compass that could guide their adherents from generation to generation. Socratic thinking lacks this. It allows for thinking untroubled by a moral compass. Christianity, which sat alongside Socratic thought, proved eminently malleable to slavery, capitalism, empire-building, fighting wars and whatever other development occurred.'

'Whoa, hold on, Olga, this is all a bit from left field. I am not sure I can cope with such a mental overload. As I see it, you are saying that Socratic thought lacked morality, and was easy picking for greedy capitalists. So, what about acquisitiveness in western society generally?'

'Acquisitiveness readily became the new god in this context, often hand in hand with Socratic thinking and Christianity, and deriving its justification from them.'

'So the western societies, with their colonial offshoots, acquire and acquire and poison and poison until there is no turning back?'

'Well, a bit like you, these thoughts are not well developed, and are a bit random. But I think there is something there. Certainly, I like to challenge the western idea that there is only one way of living, and that the West simply follows what is normal and human. I think history suggests the contrary.'

'On the face of it, you appear to be right. Africa has also avoided modern acquisitiveness for all its very long life, until very recent times. These are based on its own traditions, but somewhere these traditions have got lost during the days of the European empires.'

'With luck, we will find people who know the traditions, and they can return in the new world that is about to be born.'

'I'm with you there.'

. . . .

Johann and Olga

Johann and Olga are sitting down to a bowl of vegetable soup the following evening.

'When my head went into a wild spin and I ended up sat in a weird spaceship, I had no idea it would end up like this,' he says.

'Me neither,' says Olga. 'It's very strange how it has all worked out. Very strange.'

'And here we are in Tanzania? Is this nearly the end of this extraordinary story?' asks Johann.

'I'm not sure if it is for me,' says Olga quietly, 'I may…'

'Hey, Olga, Johann, we've found you! Bloody amazing!' It is Souad, with Abdul and Mohammed.

'Incredible, Souad, Abdul, you got here! Despite everything! Welcome, welcome, welcome,' says Johann.

'Who's this man who looks a bit like you, Abdul — not a brother perhaps?' asks Olga.

'Mohammed, yes, my brother, but he doesn't speak any English,' replies Abdul.

'Hello,' says Mohammed.

'*Salaam Alekom*,' says Olga.

They all embrace each other with wide smiles.

'It's been like living a nightmare,' says Abdul. 'We have witnessed thousands of deaths along the way. It's like one may imagine the plague in medieval times. Sheer hell. Very few people have survived anywhere.'

'Fortunately,' adds Souad, 'our Arabic helped us much of the way, and we avoided somehow dying from botulism. The Nile, thankfully, remained botulism free, and we found a rowing boat and rowed our way up the Nile very slowly all the way through Egypt, Sudan and Uganda to Lake Victoria, though we had to carry the boat a few times, with the dam and plenty of rapids.'

'Damned heavy, carrying a boat past a dam!' exclaims Abdul, half-jokingly. 'But we managed it. On the river, there was a rag-taggle collection of boats, some homemade, with people doing their best to make their way upstream. I suspect many did not make it, though, as it was really tough.'

Mohammed moves his arms like a crocodile snapping its jaws shut.

'Yes, as Mohammed indicates, a crocodile took quite a liking to us, and snapped at my arm as I rowed. It was really hairy. But then it went after the boat behind us. I heard screams, but I didn't dare look.

'Then we walked mostly. We had hibiscus juice and fresh coconut milk to drink, and fresh bananas, and bread occasionally. Otherwise, we were just very fortunate, as botulism is everywhere, and by a miracle we escaped it.

'Outside Tanzania, at the border, it looked like we may die for lack of food and drink. It was desperate there. People were fighting for the pieces of bread or fruit that were brought by newcomers.'

'But when they allowed us in,' adds Souad, 'we only had to mention the tall robot ant and someone would have heard of Eleg and would direct us. That's how we found you.'

'Fantastic!' Exclaims Olga, 'It's so good to see you again. I won't ask about what you went through on Howl until you wish to talk about it.'

'I'm not pregnant,' says Souad.

'Brilliant news!' says Olga. 'But why don't you have some soup for now? You look like you need some sustenance. Later, we can tell you about the plans for a new world in Tanzania. Life starts afresh.'

They sit down to eat, all wearing broad smiles.

...

Mathabo

Mathabo arrives with ox and cart. She collapses for a moment from exhaustion, then gathers up the energy for one more effort. She tidies the straw on her woodworm-riddled seat and takes a handful of fodder from a bag tied under her seat. She gives this to the grateful ox, then moves on.

Fortunately, she soon finds a group of people who speak Sotho.

She addresses them: 'I was at home, doing my usual chores. I went to the nearby village for thread, and all there were dead, and insects were swarming over all the houses. I went to the next village. All were dead there too, and again insects were everywhere. A car on the road had a driver dead at the wheel. The passengers were also dead. There were insects all over the bodies inside, and the seats.'

'Dear mama,' one says, 'through all this you are alive.'

'I survived somehow, in my remote hut. I took the ox, also still alive, and our cart, as I cannot walk far. We have travelled for 40 days to reach here. In both South Africa and Mozambique there was nobody on the roads except a few elderly people like me, struggling with a stick or a horse and cart. Cars were abandoned all along the road. Towns are like ghost towns.

'I brought one elderly woman with me. When we reached Tanzania, the border seemed open. There were no guards. There seemed to be more people in this country than further south.

'We were encouraged to head north for the Serengeti area, which we did. I have been asking the same question all the way.

'The question I have is a strange one perhaps: I am looking for a Swedish man named Johann. He may be about 30 years old. He will look African, like me.'

A young woman in the group says: 'A dusky European woman and an ant-shaped robot have been seen with a Sotho-looking man who does not speak African languages.'

'But I guess the chance of this being my Johann is so remote,' says Mathabo.

'Of course,' says the woman, 'but you may ask for a mixed white-Asian woman called Olga, and an ant robot. I don't know the name of the man. But you never know, perhaps he knows your Johann, or knows someone who knows him.'

Mathabo climbs back on the ox cart and heads further north. It is a very faint hope, but hope to cling on to nonetheless, like a lemur with sick baby attached.

At the next village, she asks around. One or two people mention the European woman and the ant robot, and the Sotho-looking man with them. One elderly woman says that she saw them heading east. She says there is a village about half a day further to the east at walking pace.

Once again, Mathabo climbs awkwardly on to her cart, her limbs creaking more as the journey progresses.

At the next settlement, few people speak Sotho, but when she finds a family group with familiar clothes, and asks, their eyes light up with recognition.

'The European woman and her robot are staying at a house near here. There is a man with them also, who may have Sotho blood, from his looks, but I have not heard him speak.

Go left and then right from here and look for a house with multi-coloured beads over the entrance, and a green flag. Ask for Moreen.'

A few minutes later, Mathabo stops outside the house with multicoloured beads. The European woman is there, and the robot, standing outside. It is the robot that is able to speak Sotho.

'I am looking for a man from Sweden, by the name of Johann. I understand that there is a man with you who speaks European languages. I am hoping he may know Johann.'

Eleg translates for Olga, and then says:

'We have a man named Johann with us.'

Olga says: 'Johann is Swedish, and he says he is originally from southern Africa.' Eleg translates.

'You mean that the man with you is called Johann, and he is from Sweden?'

'Yes,' says Eleg, 'why do you wish to know?'

'I gave birth to a boy, 42 years ago, she says. A Swedish family adopted him because we were all dying of Aids or leprosy.'

Olga screams, on hearing Eleg's translation: 'You are Johann's mother! You must be. I can see it in your eyes now. Incredible! Unbelievable!'

'You Braibies are strange,' says Eleg.

'Shut up, for once, Eleg. This is good news. We must find Johann. Please translate for me.'

As Eleg translates, Moreen arrives. 'Some people have attacked Johann, she says. One had a knife. Didn't like him being European. He is badly hurt. We need to get medical aid to him quickly. But who are you?' she asks, turning to Mathabo.

'Do you speak any Sotho?'

'A little. I may understand.'

'I am searching for my son Johann. I believe he may be the Johann who is staying with you.'

'Oh my God! Johann's mother! We must go there. He is badly hurt,' warns Moreen.

Eleg lifts Mathabo and holds her with his upper legs, and walks on his lower legs, with Olga and Moreen alongside.

There is a crowd, and blackish-red blood trickling by someone's legs. Mathabo shouts 'Johann!' and Eleg puts her down. She hobbles straight to Johann, with Olga alongside.

His head is flopped to the side, his curly hair caked with blood. More blood is seeping from a deep wound in his thigh. It is not clear if he is alive.

Mathabo collapses on to her knees by him, distraught, staring into his face.

Eleg holds up a middle leg and fires some sticky green liquid at the wound in Johann's head. 'This will stop up the wound,' says Eleg, in English.

Olga stoops by Mathabo and feels Johann's pulse. It is faint.

'There are no functioning medical services,' explains Moreen.

'I will carry Johann to your house,' says Eleg, addressing Moreen in Swahili.

He lifts Johann and cradles him in his upper legs. Moreen helps Mathabo back to the house, supporting her shoulder as she walks, while Olga walks alongside Eleg.

'He is my son,' says Mathabo, 'I see it in his eyes. They are the eyes of our family. I am in a tither, both elated at finding him here, and deeply anxious about his bad injury.'

'I do understand,' says Moreen, squeezing her hand.

At the house, Eleg places Johann on Olga's bed. His head wound is no longer open, with Eleg's green liquid covering the area. Olga looks for some cloth, and tears some to make a tourniquet.

'You have helped his head,' says Olga to Eleg. 'But his leg looks in a really bad way. I am putting on this tourniquet to try to stop the blood loss, though I fear it is too late. Can you do anything?'

'The wound is deep,' says Eleg, 'I will spray on some of my coagulant, but I suspect that in a human there is artery damage that needs to be dealt with,' and he sprays some green liquid on the wound.

As Moreen and Mathabo enter, Olga says: 'I am seriously worried about Johann. I think he may die if we do not take urgent action. But I am not sure what action to take. Is there a medical person in the village, perhaps?'

'Two doors down is a woman who was a doctor,' says Moreen. 'I will see if she will come.'

Mathabo kneels next to Johann's bed in tears, holding his hand. Johann remains silent and seems unconscious.

'I will have a look at him,' says the doctor, coming into the bedroom. Mathabo and Olga move aside.

After a few minutes, she says: 'I have no idea what this strange substance is, but it has stemmed the blood loss for the moment. The tourniquet has helped too. But I am deeply concerned that the patient will die if we do not remove his leg.

'There is a real danger of septicaemia, and this could mean rapid death if it takes hold. As such, we need to do this soon.'

Eleg explains to Olga, and also Johann, assuming he can hear. Moreen explains in Sotho to Mathabo.

'I agree,' says Mathabo.

'Do you have a saw, perhaps, or a sharp knife?' asks Olga, turning to Moreen. 'And plenty of hot water?'

'I think I have a knife that will be sharp enough,' says Moreen, 'but I will need help from neighbours with the water.'

'I can help with water,' says the doctor. 'My name is Neema, by the way.'

'I will use the knife. I can cut through in seconds,' says Eleg. 'I suggest the doctor stays to help with the cleaning, and to stop up the wound. I will use my coagulant. You others do not have the stomach for this, I believe.'

'I agree. I will take Mathabo out, and Moreen,' says Olga.

Mathabo insists she wants to stay, but Moreen persuades otherwise, and they go to Neema's house.

Neema meanwhile prepares two buckets of hot water, and a tighter tourniquet. She also finds some ultra-strong painkillers at her home, but fears that these will not be enough. She also brings clean rags, a felt tip pen and fairly thin rod of wood, the latter for Johann's teeth to grip on to when the pain is at its most intense.

The buckets of hot water are ready, and Neema checks the new tourniquet.

As soon as Neema places the rod in Johann's mouth, and marks with the felt tip pen the precise place to cut, Eleg uses his two upper feet to make three powerful cuts with the knife. On the third cut, the leg severs at the upper thigh.

Johann's whole body shakes, and he screams silently but forcefully through the wooden rod.

Neema washes carefully around the wound and stands back while Eleg fires some of his green coagulant at the gaping wound. Neema then uses the rags to bind the wound, while the blood solidifies with the coagulant.

She feels Johann's pulse. It is still weak, but there is a slight improvement. She checks Johann's temperature, and nods.

She holds Johann, who moans quietly. She nods to Eleg: 'You are not bad for a robot,' she says.

'You are not bad for a Braiby,' he replies.

'Braiby, what is that?'

'It was Olga's phrase. In English, it is short for Brainless Brainies, which sums up an intelligent species that so seriously damages its Blue Planet home, that it makes it almost uninhabitable.'

She laughs. 'I like that,' she says. 'It says everything about how we got to this situation.'

'My masters needed to take action to protect their ant cousins here, and millions of other species.'

'Well, I can't agree with the nature of the action taken, with most humans killed. But in a strange way I do understand, even though it should be against all my principles.'

'It is done.'

She laughs. 'You are so brutally matter-of-fact. But you are of course correct. It is done,' and she checks Johann's pulse again. 'You know, I think Johann may just survive.'

'Braibies are weak creatures,' says Eleg.

'In some ways, we are. I will fetch his mother, and the others.'

Mathabo is overjoyed, and thanks Neema as she hugs Johann's chest, and sheds tears of happiness. Olga smiles at Eleg.

'You are a funny old thing,' she says to Eleg, 'you take part in killing billions, and save one.'

'I seem to be becoming a bit too like a Braiby,' replies Eleg. 'I better watch that.'

Over the following days, Mathabo spends day and night with Johann, as he experiences fits, and a ferocious fever. Neema tries her best with the few medicines that she can get her hands on.

Eventually, on the sixth day after the leg amputation, Johann opens his eyes and says: 'Hello, Mum.'

Mathabo hugs him, and kisses his lips, then says (with Moreen translating): 'I have to apologise to you, my darling son. All your brothers and sisters had died. We wanted you to live, but this meant that we could not keep you.'

'You do not need to apologise. I understand. I am very pleased to meet you.'

He cries, and tears run down her cheeks They hug each other tightly and stay that way until Mathabo feels she must sit down.

That night, Mathabo dies peacefully in her sleep. Johann attends her burial the next day, using a pair of walking sticks he has borrowed, and tanked up on painkillers. He sheds a Lake Victoria tributary of tears as he does so.

...

Olga, Abdul and Moreen

'I don't understand where culture fits into the new world,' says Abdul.

'There is no blueprint. We are embarking on a new way of living. Anyone can put forward their ideas,' says Olga in response.

'Eleg and Reson say that culture, as we understand it, has no place in the ant world. Can it have a place in our world?'

'Absolutely! There are at present no rules, except that we will no longer live in a way that damages the planet. Do you want to try to put some ideas together, and float them round?'

'I am more concerned to preserve great works of literature and drama, of art and music. Some of this, especially art and music, may be impractical, at least for now.'

'Dar es Salaam,' says Moreen, 'has the Tanzanian National Library with great works from Africa, India, the Middle East, Europe, China, the USA etc. Like Abdul, I would like to find a way of preserving these for this generation and future generations.'

'Nobody will stand in your way, either of you,' says Olga. 'Why don't you put together a team of like-minded people? There are bound to be many here.'

'Will Dar be safe?' asks Abdul.

'The ants bearing the botulism bacteria will no longer be in Dar,' continues Olga, 'as Tanzania is being left free to grow again. I suspect it will not be safe to go for several days, but even then, you should only eat fresh food and drink bottled drinks. Perhaps, you could go in a few days and find out what is still there, and what state it is in. Beware of groups of survivors desperate for food. We don't know how people will react to the new circumstances.'

'Makes sense,' says Moreen. 'I have heard a number of reports of groups of people in small towns raiding stores and depots for food. It may be worse in Dar.'

'When you find out more about what's been preserved, you can perhaps have a discussion with like-minded people about where this fits in with the priorities here,' says Olga. 'Personally, I may not be here.'

'I will be happy to join in the discussion, and I know others who may fit the bill for this too. I will also join you on a trip to Dar, Abdul, as I know where the library is.'

'What about energy — to maintain air-conditioning in a library in this climate?' asks Abdul. 'What forms of energy will this new society use?'

'Solar and wind energy, as well as hydro, tidal and other forms of renewable energy, will be favoured in particular.'

'There is already a solar and wind power industry here, and also hydro,' says Moreen. 'There was a Tanzanian Renewable Energy Association in Arusha. We could go there also, and see if there are any survivors there, or any connections that can be followed up.'

'I suspect that there will also be a question of priorities,' suggests Olga. 'No doubt the hospitals in Dar es Salaam and Arusha will be a priority for energy, where supply is limited, and others will make a claim for energy needs also. In time, some form of new decision-making process will no doubt take shape, and it should become easier to make decisions for the new society here. But nothing is fixed, within certain parameters. You can all have an important role to play.'

'I am pleased that culture will have a place,' says Abdul. 'I may get together some singers and musicians and arrange a small festival. We need some happiness and a sense of coming together after all the extraordinary and heart-rending change that has happened.'

'Great idea, Abdul. Let's do it!' exclaims Moreen enthusiastically.

...

Olga and Eleg

'Galaloop,' says Eleg.

'What did you say?' asks Olga, eyebrows heading south.

'I'm trying to gulp like a human.'

'You are a hoot sometimes, my dear. You say the most unlikely things. You can't gulp because you have no larynx that can rise up and down.'

'Can I say "galaloop"?'

'Yes, you can, you crackpot crane of a robot.'

'Ah, crane again. Very good.'

'But tell me why you want to say "galaloop"?'

'I want to try something with you, but I am nervous about it.'

'No robot in his right mind gets nervous.'

'Well, maybe you have knocked the nail on its bonce.'

'Hit the nail on its head.'

'Is that not the same?'

'It's just that the phrase is "to hit the nail on the head".'

'OK. Logged.'

'What do you want to try?'

'If I put a middle leg up here (and it lifts its middle leg) by the side of your face, touching just below your earlobe, it should give you positive energy, just like it does for ants.'

'Is this the right spot?' and she holds the end of its middle leg by her cheek.

'Let it nestle just below your earlobe there, that is fine.'

'Should I feel something?'

'Try to wait a little.'

'There is a bit of a tingle. Ooh, wow, oh my God. This is a bit yum.'

'Shall I stop?'

'Heaven no, Eleg. This is the most fun I've had in a very long time.'

'I'd better stop.'

'Heh, heh, not so fast. Just leave it there a little longer. Mmm. Is this really something that you do to ants?'

'Would you mind if I had told a bit of a fib?'

'You are a bit of a rogue at times, a very big rogue even. But a lovable one.'

And Eleg eventually pulls its leg down, with Olga curling up in a ball, savouring the sensations she feels.

Chapter 10
Trumbushton and Xi Ji Ping on Howl

The carriage is stationary.

In front, two near naked men, with in each case a bull horn over his groin, pointing upwards. They argue.

'I am not pushing this fucking cart.'

'You will be punished if you do not, as will I.'

'They can do what they want. My men will come, and we will wreak revenge on all these weirdo robots, the ants and whatever else they throw at us.'

'The robot is coming.'

'Pretend to push, Jee.'

And they pick up the wooden bar and start leaning into it to move the carriage.

'You have not moved,' says the robot, named Adam. 'I will need to punish you.'

'We are moving,' says Trumbushton. 'If you paralyse us, we cannot move.'

The robot emits the white gooey stuff in their direction, to stick on their necks.

'Fucking hell,' says Trumbushton. 'I've never been so humiliated in all my life. Or in such damn pain.' And he rubs his neck with his right hand, to try to soothe it, but it does not help. It just makes the fingers of his hand rigid and stuck together.

'We are both in the same boat,' says Xi. 'We chose to come here, not knowing that indeed there is a superior breed of ants.'

'I don't know about superior. I'd beat them at golf any day. Knock socks off them on the stock market.'

'I think that these would not help here on Howl. And now we both have an ambition to return to earth, but we have first to face this work pushing carriages as punishment.'

'We will never escape.'

'If we accept that they are the saviours of the earth, and that we will work for good here, and not act badly, they may let us go.'

'I will never do that.'

'So you will spend the rest of your days pushing this cart on an alien planet.'

'For each person who begins to weep somewhere else another stops. The same is true of the laugh.'

'Who says that?' asks Xi

'My wife Melania quotes it to me. Can't think why I remembered it. Think a guy called Peckett, Buckett, or Beckett wrote it.'

'Samuel Beckett?'

'Could be, who knows? Either way, this is us. I moan and complain, and you stop moaning and complaining. Probably if you moan and complain, I will stop.'

'I have something that fits too.'

'What's that?'

'I'm going to quote some words of Bob Dylan at you.'

'Spare me. I hate, loathe and detest that long haired Commie so and so, I've told you that before.'

Xi sings: 'Even the President of the United States sometimes has to stand naked.'

'Shit. Did he sing that? I suppose you like it that the running dog President is naked as the day he was born.'

'That was a different China. We are different today. We don't talk of running dogs. We try to like the USA and do business with you.'

'Yea, while you take over the world, bit by bit, with nobody watching.'

'I do not think we can survive being on Howl if you speak like this.'

'I don't have to like you, Jee.'

'You could tolerate me.'

'Like a goat in the backyard?'

'No, as a neighbour who is not a friend but who you need to get along with.'

'I had that once.'

'Please think about it.'

'I will.'

'Just shut your eyes for a moment, President. Just imagine that every word is like an unnecessary stain on silence and nothingness. Think about that. It is Beckett again.'

'You want me to shut the fuck up.'

'I do, but that is not what this means. It means that silence has a value too. Words that have no place are a stain on that silence. Let us try to use our words more wisely.'

'What, so we kowtow to these monsters?'

'No, you are jumping to wrong conclusions again. I am talking about finding a way to get through today. And if we get through today, we try to get through tomorrow, and so on.'

'Well, for a Commie, you do at times speak sense, Jee. Maybe I need to get off my high horse.'

'It would be a start.'

'Am I a mighty pain in the ass.'

'President, the sage Confucius says: "A man who has committed a mistake and doesn't correct it is committing a further mistake." Will you think about this? And, no, you are not a pain in anything.'

'This is a lot of philosophy for one day, goddammit!'

'Please think about it. On the spaceship, we would not back down on the demands of the ants, when we could have returned to earth. We are now stuck here on this planet as mere labourers unless we display wisdom and learn from the mistake we made.'

'Heavy.'

'But true. Please do not dismiss this.'

'I'll tell you tomorrow what I think. I may need some shuteye first.'

'Shuteye?'

'Sleep.'

'Understood.'

'Where did you learn Beckett in Red China, Jee?'

'In all the years when nothing seemed to change, many of us read Beckett's *Waiting for Godot*. In Mandarin, of course. In quiet moments. It seemed to sum up very well our situation.'

'Last book I read was Huck Finn.'

'Nothing else?'

'Well, *Playboy*, I guess. They have some good stories.'

'I don't know this *Playboy*.'

'No, I don't imagine that such magazines got past the censor in your country. They probably had too much fun leafing through it in the censor's office.'

'I think my English doesn't stretch so far.'

'Well, can we get off this goddam wagon and get our heads down for the night? What do you say?'

Xi calls Adam: 'Hey, AdamAnt, when do we get to stop, and go to bed for the night?'

Adam replies, 'You have done a little better today. I will let you go to your cabin now. But you will do more hours tomorrow.'

'That's not what I hoped to hear, more work,' says Trumbushton, as they head up to their cabin.

'Start here, Mr President. Think of tomorrow as another day, one day nearer our freedom.'

'Shit, taking lessons from a Commie. They'd never believe it back home. A Commie that snores, too.'

'I will lie on my side. My wife says I snore less then.'

They reach the cabin, and head in.

'Goddamit, you're a sly one, Jee. I didn't know you had a wife.'

'She is called Peng Liyuan. She was a folk singer but is now retired.'

'Well I'll be. But, Jee, just don't start singing her songs, for pity's sake.'

'Well, we can do a deal, you spare me your songs, and I will spare you my wife's.'

'Let's shake on that, Jee jinping,' and they shake.

And go to bed.

...

After breakfast, Trumbushton says:

'You are a sly son of a bitch, Jee.'

'This is a favourite phrase of yours. Why do you say that, President?'

'You hate these ants and this planet as much as me, but you work out a way to try to escape.'

'If one has a pain in the stomach, one does not want that pain tomorrow.'

'That Confucius again?'

'No, just me. Common sense. Will you agree to pretend to get along with our new masters?'

'I'll sure try. You may need to remind me from time to time.'

'And we agree that our aim is to try to get back on that spaceship and find a way home?'

'Yes indeedy, comrade.'

'Ah, comrade, now is it? Friend would do for me?'

'Jee.'

'President?'

'You mentioned Laurel and Hardy back on the ship.'

'I did.'

'I think I can work with saying, like Oliver Hardy: "I might look like I'm doing it, but in my mind I am not."'

'Perfect! We may escape this planet yet.'

Chapter 11
Eleg and Olga Head Back to Howl

1. Tanzania Farewell

'Guys, I am staying put in Tanzania,' says Johann, 'I will learn one or two new languages and try to help in whatever small ways I can in creating the new Tanzania.'

'The same goes with me,' says Souad.

'Remember what we talked about, Johann,' says Eleg.

'Yes, the huts to be generally built with natural materials, depending on the locality. Use local knowledge and experience in every case, if it is available and practical; don't reinvent the wheel, or the baobab tree; no plastics, no electronics, no metals.'

'You've some memory, Johann.'

'Thanks. Also, some huts to be traditional twig structure, sometimes filled in with planks, but mostly with mud; rooves to be grass or, if available, palm leaves; some may have mainly interwoven twigs for the walls, with woven mats on the inside for extra warmth, depending on what grows in the area, and what the weather is like locally. Higher areas will have colder nights. I've gone through it with locals, and all that stuff is fine with me.

'A bit tougher will be people who had got used to city life needing to adapt to subsistence farming, husbandry, traditional skills etc., with some trading in simple goods.'

'Abdul, Mohammed and I will recruit people who can help,' says Souad. 'There will be many willing, I am sure.'

'Sure,' says Abdul. And Mohammed nods.

'We need to think about our new society,' says Moreen. 'We will need to try to ensure that this small population that remains starts off in the right way and does not revert to old ways.'

'Yes, but I think not by compulsion,' suggests Olga, 'but by example, education, and encouragement. Don't you have a long tradition of cooperation in Tanzania, of the individual working for the collective whole?'

'We do. We have Ujamaa, which was the way we lived in the first decades after independence, which did emphasise the individual working for the collective whole. Although many things changed, and Ujamaa was abandoned. We became more individualistic, but there are many indications that this principle is still part of our people's culture and can be fostered again.'

'Individuals working towards a common goal, as part of a collective whole, sounds a good starting point,' suggests Johann. 'You can build from there. The new society can then slowly evolve in its own way.'

'All a bit idealistic,' says Moreen. 'But I take your point. I think I will need to bring my administrative skills to bear, to get a few basic things in place: everybody having shelter, having access to food and drink, and having a chance to contribute. With that in place, which may take a while, we can start thinking about seeing what public buildings can still be used, whether hospitals, schools or public administration, and see who we have left in the way of professional people with skills. It's going to a be a long and interesting road.'

'It seems to be in good hands.' says Johann.

Across the way, a woman with a mobile phone has it taken off her by an officious looking man, who says: 'All networks are dead now, so mobiles are defunct. We are collecting them all in.'

'Olga, you are not staying, are you?' asks Johann.

'I think it is clear where I am at Johann. I want to return to Howl,' says Olga.

'Can I ask you something?'

'Try me,' says *Olga*.

'You now know as much about my origins as I do,' says Johann to Olga.

'I do,' says Olga, 'quite a surprise!'

'Can you tell me a bit more about yours?'

'I s'pose. I think I told you my mum was from Bangalore, India. My dad was mixed Danish-German. They were both working with refugees in different parts of the Middle East, after one crisis followed another. They met in Damascus, they tell me, in a little café where refugee workers sometimes met. I was born in Damascus, but then lived in India until my teens, when I came to Europe with my father.'

'Maybe that's why you seem quite worldly.'

'Don't be deceived. My parents split up when I was in my teens. I lived mostly in Copenhagen, then England, with just a few short visits to India.'

'Husband, wife, boyfriend, girlfriend?'

'All those! No, I joke. There was for a while this guy Ned, from northern England, Berwick-upon-Tweed.'

'Not heard of it.'

'Never mind. He was a troubled soul, like so many. Mental health issues. But a nice guy. I liked him a lot.'

'Could it have become serious?'

'I don't know. I might have had a baby with him, if I hadn't been taken to the spaceship when I was, but I don't know about Ned as a father. I guess the proof is usually in the pudding, and the pudding never happened.'

'And now you will never know.'

'Too true. But I think the time has come. I think Eleg wants to do his disappearing trick.'

'With you?'

'With me, of course.'

'It's been very special knowing you, very good indeed.'

'It's been magic knowing you too, peg leg, whether with two legs or with one.'

'Maybe you will come back. You never know.'

'But I will be so much older.'

'Age is immaterial. It's the person underneath.'

They embrace.

Abdul and Souad come across and embrace Olga also. They shout 'Bye Big Bird' to Eleg.

'We are going. Stand here,' orders Eleg, coaxing Olga to stand right in front of him. He presses two buttons on a panel on his right front leg.

They disappear.

….

2. Eleg and Olga on Spaceship Back to Howl

Olga and Eleg arrive on the reserve spaceship.

'Are we returning to Howl?' asks Olga.

'Yes,' says Eleg.

'I am happy to live there now, with you.'

'Of course,' says Eleg.

'It's quiet.'

'There is only one other robot on the ship, and no bees. No other Braibies this time.'

'What about fuel?'

'Fuel?'

'You told the Braibies on the first trip that their bodies would be used for fuel, to get the spaceship home.'

'It's my programming. I can't help my programming. My masters like to make it hard for the Braibies mentally, to turn the knife in a bit deeper, I think you say.'

'A bit of a grudge?'

'My masters don't have emotions like Braibies do. But the way that the Braibies have damaged the Blue Planet and threatened the lives of so many ants on the planet has brought out an emotion not normally expressed. It's a species remembered emotion going back to the monkeys.'

'So none of the bodies were used for fuel.'

'No, but the cockroaches were well fed.'

'Ow! Serves me right for asking.'

'You are not normally so squeamish.'

'True. I'm slipping. But allow me some human emotion. Time to sleep?' asks Olga.

'Come. I will take you to the cryogenics machine.'

'You have such a wicked way with you, my dear,' she jests, as she steps in.

'If only you knew,' says Eleg. And he closes the lid.

. . .

As they head back to Howl, there is a glitch in the ship's bearings.

The very precise surfing between two Black Holes, to break out of the limitations of the speed of light, does not proceed as planned this time.

Instead of surfing on the edge of two conjoined Black Holes, they appear to be flying towards one of the Black Holes.

Word gets to Eleg.

Eleg wakes Olga from her frozen state. She takes a while to return to a semblance of normality.

'Are we near Howl?' she asks.

'No. The spaceship has malfunctioned. It is expected to explode at any time in the next 1,000 human years, or the next 1,000 seconds. Or some point in between. We do not know which,' Eleg explains to Olga.

'You have a way of being wholly un-reassuring when you seek to be reassuring. Are we going to die?' asks Olga.

'You will, I understand. I don't live or die. Though I may go boinnng.'

'Is that a mega boiinnnnnng or a mini boinng?'

'More a mega one, I suspect.'

'What may happen to us? Do you know?'

'We are in unknown territory. It may be that the universe we have just left has been affected also and may start to go backwards in time.'

'Our universe? Where the Blue Planet is?'

'Yes, your universe.'

'Backwards, so human lives go backwards?

'Yes, that is possible.'

'Wow, that could solve the problem of climate change in an unexpected way.'

'Possibly, but there are many imponderables.'

'And older people would become younger, much to their enjoyment.'

'Possibly, but babies would shrivel into tiny foetuses and wither into nothing, just a limp sperm and redundant egg.'

'Not that positive then?'

'Gravity is the conductor of the orchestra here, and it largely determines.'

'Wow, what next in this jack in a box? Tell me a bit about gravity then, Eleg. I never got past an apple falling.'

'Gravity is the great creator, and a great destroyer. After the Great Awakening...'

'The what?'

'You call it the Big Bang, I understand, although there might never have been a bang sound.'

'OK, so after the Great Awakening?'

'There were billions of rocks and bits of matter spreading ever outwards into the universe. Gravity pulled these together to form stars and planets, including your sun, your moon, your Earth, our Howl, and all the stars and planets.'

'Amazing, but it destroys too?'

'Gravity is also the force at the heart of the Black Hole and here it is such an insuperably powerful force that it is able to draw stars into it such that they become ex-stars. Gravity may also be the force now dragging us to the heart of the Black Hole.'

'So gravity is Dr Jekyll and Mr Hyde. It is a force for good and also a force for destruction.'

'I don't know the reference, but in a nutshell that is right.'

'So might we disappear?'

'It may reassure you that mass cannot disappear.'

'Mass?'

'Stuff, anything imaginable, but mainly the building blocks of what is in space. That includes us. We cannot disappear.'

'OK.'

'As mass cannot disappear it tends to find a home. This will be the case with us, most likely. Either way, we should find a home, but perhaps not the one we expect.'

'If nothing else, Eleg, you have led me to expect the unexpected on this journey together. You know, they say that death is the big joke that life is playing on us. I am ready for anything.'

'Morbid joke, you have. The "not disappearing rule" does not necessarily apply in one very special case, I am sorry to say.'

'Uh, oh. This is where you give me the bad news.'

'Your universe could be swallowed up by a Black Hole and cease to exist for any meaningful purpose. It would be so minute that it would be beyond detection.'

'Somehow, Eleg, this is all so big and abstract it sort of passes me by. But if we may shrink to nothing, can we at least stay together until then?'

'I am not going anywhere, apart from into the complete unknown, so I think so.'

'I mean, can we be close together? Close and personal. A superior kind of complete unknown.'

'Of course, we can. You know my thoughts about you.'

'If my mother could hear me, about to elope with an ant robot, she'd go off her rocker.'

'Is that bad or good?'

'Bad, usually. But she would never stand in my way, my mother.'

'She may be worried about your half-grown eyebrows.'

'Oh my God, they have never fully grown back since the horrid mealworms, have they?'

'It makes you more like me, eyebrow-less.'

'Eyebrow-less in Gaza.'

'In Gaza?'

'It's a pun on a movie title?'

'My sensors are picking something up.'

'Your sensible serendipitous sensuous sensors. What are you getting?'

'We might not be plummeting into Armageddon after all.'

'You have such a dry way of announcing spectacular news.'

'It seems we may have been spat out.'

'Story of my life.'

'I think I may need to freeze you, as it could be eons before we know for sure"

'Eons? You like to keep a girl waiting, don't you?'

"I want you to be alive when I know for certain whether or not you are dead."

"You could tax a great philosopher with that one."

'It is all too imponderable, it is better you are frozen, as time could become highly elastic, and the human body does not react well to bendy time.'

'Point taken, but can you give me a little time before I go into the freezer like frozen pizza Margherita, Eleg?'

'We may not have a lot of time, Olga.'

'Or we may have plenty of time.'

'Sadly, time is not elastic in that way.'

'Sure, Eleg, but you can give me a few moments as they may be our last? Could you do that thing where you place one of your front legs against the place near my earlobe?'

'I can,' and Eleg places his favoured massage leg in her preferred position.

'Mmmmm. When you do that, I could love you always.'

'I could love you too. Correction. I do love you.'

'Can you do this forever?'

'Forever is a very long word.'

'And a very short one.'

'It is.'

'So is life.'